The Laws of the State of Nevada Affecting Church Property

This dissertation was approved by the Rev. John J. McGrath, A.B., LL.B., J.C.D., Professor of Civil and Comparative Law, as director and the by the Rev. John Rogg Schmidt, A.B., LL.B., J.C.D., and the Rev. Fredrick R. McManus, A.B., J.C.D., as readers.

THE CATHOLIC UNIVERSITY OF AMERICA
CANON LAW STUDIES
No. 409

The Laws of the State of Nevada Affecting Church Property

A DISSERTATION

Submitted to the Faculty of the School of Canon Law of The Catholic University of America in Partial Fulfillment of the Requirements for the Degree of Doctor of Canon Law

BY

MAURICE L. WELSH, A.B., M.A., J.C.L.
Priest of the Diocese of Reno

THE CATHOLIC UNIVERSITY OF AMERICA PRESS
WASHINGTON, D.C.
1962

Nihil Obstat:

JOHN J. MCGRATH, A.B., LL.B., J.C.D.
Censor Deputatus

Washingtonii, D.C., die 27 *aprilis,* 1959

Imprimatur:

+ ROBERT J. DWYER, D.D., PH.D.
Episcopus Renensis

Renensi, die 18 *januarii,* 1961

Printed by
JAY BARKER COMPANY, INC.
Reno, Nevada

TO MY MOTHER

FOREWORD

Nevada is a state large in area, sparse in population. Part of the fresh, mushrooming Far West of the United States, it is a region characterized more by its sharp, optimistic eye for the future than by any unyielding veneration for the past. Nevada is young, and so is the Catholic Church there.

Nevadans are known as an independent, confident, hospitable, stouthearted people. They have gladly welcomed all who have sought to make their homes and earn their livelihood in the rugged country of the state—welcomed, and more than that, lent a helping hand.

Such, too, has been the story of Church and State in Nevada. It has been a quiet, peaceful tale, unsullied by battles and discord such as have marked the efforts at co-existence between these two perfect societies in so many parts of the world. Nevada has welcomed religion and lent it all the support possible within the framework of the federal constitution. Churches have been able to grow and flourish in Nevada's communities, and have been extended a respect and gratitude that must rank as outstanding among the states in the Union.

One aspect of the Church-State relationship in Nevada is the burden of this work. This study will concern itself with the laws of the state of Nevada which affect the property holding of churches. The plan of the work is to present a brief history of the civil and ecclesiastical development of the state. Against the background of the story of its beginnings, Nevada's legislation is better understood. Since Nevada, along with all the other states in the Union, recognizes the legal personality of churches only through incorporation according to the laws of the state, the second part of this work will review the various corporation laws of Nevada. The third section, and main body of the study, will treat the question of the acquisition, tenure, and administration of church property. The method followed here will be to outline the regulations of the canon law of the Catholic Church on each of these points first, and then present the corresponding civil laws of Nevada, drawing appropriate comparisons and contrasts between the two bodies of legislation. It is hoped that the study may prove of some value to ecclesiastics, attorneys, judges, and legislators in our state.

The writer wishes to express warm thanks to His Excellency, the Most Reverend Robert J. Dwyer, D.D., Ph.D., Bishop of Reno, for providing the opportunity to undertake graduate studies in Canon Law. He is grateful to the members of the Faculty of the School of Canon Law of the Catholic University of America for their generous assistance during the course of these studies and in the preparation of this work. Particular thanks are in order to his dissertation director, the Rev. John J. McGrath, LL.B., J.C.D. and to Nevada attorneys Paul Laxalt and Russell McDonald and their staffs for indispensable help in the civil law involved in the work.

TABLE OF CONTENTS

CHAPTER III

CHAPTER IV

CHAPTER I

HISTORY OF NEVADA: ECCLESIASTICAL AND CIVIL

Long after America's Atlantic Coast had been settled by the pilgrim fathers, half a century after the revolutionists had declared and won this nation's independence, long after the hardy Franciscan Friars had tramped the arduous *El Camino Real* along the Pacific's coastline, long after white civilization had begun to take root in America's South, Southwest, and Midwest, Nevada was still unknown to the white man.

Nevertheless, as "one born out of due time," Nevada became the thirty-sixth of the fifty states to be admitted into the Union. Indeed, it took just thirteen years after the first house was completed in Nevada for it to become a state. A combination of war, silver, a strong, independent attitude, and keen, political leadership blended to achieve this sudden coming into statehood in contrast to the customary, gradual development of so many of the states.

It was not until 1826 that the first white man journeyed into that territory which is now Nevada. It was not until 1851 that the first white men settled down to make their homes in that region, though for a quarter of a century first trapper, then pathfinder, emigrant, and forty-niner in ever increasing numbers had crossed its rugged ranges and deserts to California.

But once the settlers arrived, things happened swiftly. The very same year that they dug the foundations for their new homes on the eastern slopes of the roughhewn Sierra Nevada, these first settlers, an impatient breed, established a squatter government and boldly petitioned Congress for a "distinct Territorial Government." One decade later, Nevada became a Territory. After a lapse of only three years, in 1864, it was declared a State, and, as far as the Northern States and Abraham Lincoln were concerned, immediately justified its statehood by casting the deciding votes in favor of the thirteenth amendment.

Actually, several Spanish priests from New Mexico first put Nevada on the map. In 1774, Captain Juan Bautista de Anza set out from Santa Fe, New Mexico, in search of an overland route to Monterey, California. He was accompanied by Father Francisco Garces. The Anza route did not touch Nevada, but two years later Father Garces undertook once more to explore in the region of the Colorado river and to christianize the Indians of that country. This journey brought the Spanish Franciscan to the very edge of the Nevada border, near Hoover Dam, although historians hold today that the priest did not actually enter Nevada.[1]

The same year two other Franciscan priests, Francisco Atanasio Dominguez and Silvestre Velez de Escalante, started from Santa Fe, also in quest of a direct route to California with the intention of establishing missions along the way. The party got as far as Southern Utah, but there, plagued by disputes with some of the soldiers, the loss of their Indian guide, and a snowstorm, they gave up their plans to reach California, sought out the Colorado river instead, and thence returned to Santa Fe.[2] This party, too, approached Nevada's borders but failed to enter the territory.[3]

However, from these journeys came maps, and on these maps there began to appear a river, the San Buenaventura, which flowed across Nevada and through the Sierra Nevada range to San Francisco Bay.[4] Thus the legend grew that in the "Unknown Land" there rushed a river to the sea, and interest in the "Northern Mystery" heightened.

Fur competition led to the initial probing of this mysterious land. Jedediah Strong Smith led the first expedition into Nevada in 1826.[5] A partner in the Rocky Mountain Fur Company, Smith decided to explore the trapping possibilities of this country south and west of the Great Salt Lake, around which the company's enterprises were centered. In late August of 1826, he and a party of fifteen men headed south from the Great Salt Lake to Lake Sevier. From this point they followed a more westward line and entered Nevada, probably near Panaca or Caliente, picking up the Muddy river. Now

[1] Mack, *Nevada* (Glendale, California: The Arthur H. Clark Company, 1936), pp. 59-60 (hereafter cited Mack). However, Bancroft is among those who believed that Father Garces did actually "enter within the present limits of Nevada." Cf. Bancroft, *History of Nevada, Colorado, and Wyoming* (San Francisco: The History Company, 1890), p. 27 (hereafter cited Bancroft).

[2] Mack, pp. 60-61; Morgan, *The Humboldt: Highroad of the West* (New York: Farrar and Rinehart, 1943), p. 11 (hereafter cited Morgan).

[3] Nevada was also approached, but not entered, from the west by Lieutenant Gabriel Moraga in 1819. Cf. Mack, p. 61.

[4] Bancroft reprints several of these earliest maps of the Nevada area. Cf. Bancroft, pp. 27-35.

[5] Mack, p. 62; Morgan devotes a chapter to the details of this excursion of Smith. He has also written a biography of the famous trapper. Cf. Morgan, pp. 17-26.

going almost due south through the Meadow Valley Wash to the Virgin and then the Colorado rivers, Smith crossed the southern tip of what is now Nevada into California.

His return the following spring took Smith through central Nevada. Although historians disagree on the specific route, it is most probable that Smith crossed the Sierras at Sonora Pass, forded the Walker river south of Walker Lake (which he apparently did not see), and struggled northeast through the rugged and waterless regions of Mineral, Nye, and White Pine counties into Utah.[6]

Jedediah Smith had found no beaver in Nevada, no great San Buenaventura rolling to the sea. He had not even seen the shallow Humboldt, which would soon mark the emigrant trail across the Great Basin towards California. He discovered only a terrible, sandy wasteland which demanded all there was in a man to cross. The tough pioneer, a native New Yorker and one of the far West's truly heroic figures, was the first to endure the treacherous secrets of the "Northern Mystery." Others followed to trap with success, others to blaze the short route to California's gold, and others to discover wealth in the basin's own craggy mountain ranges. But their forerunner knew nothing of this; he died too early, victim of a Comanche arrow on the Cimarron river, while enroute to Santa Fe in 1831.[7]

A competitor of Smith discovered the beaver which he had failed to find. Peter Skene Ogden, a chief trapper for the vast Hudson's Bay Company, discovered the Humboldt river in northern Nevada.[8] He called it the "Unknown River"[9] and trapped from its source to the Big Bend where it turns southward. He was followed into Nevada by many trappers—men such as Milton Sublette, Joseph Walker, Thomas McCoy, Kit Carson—who met with varying fortune in their beaver trapping but succeeded in solving more and more of the secrets of the "Unknown Land."[10]

[6] Mack, p. 66.

[7] Morgan, pp. 25-26.

[8] Mack, p. 68.

[9] This was the first of a long list of names attached to the stream. It was also known as Ogden's river, Mary's river, St. Mary's river, Paul's river. The name which has survived is that given it by John Charles Fremont, who called it the Humboldt after Baron Alexander von Humboldt, a German scientist, who never saw the stream. Cf. Morgan, pp. 5-6.

[10] Reproduction of Thompson and West, *History of Nevada,* (Berkeley: Howell and North, 1881) with Illustrations and Biographical Sketches of its Prominent Men and Pioneers. (Berkeley: Howell and North, 1958), p. 22 (hereafter cited Thompson-West).

A notable expedition across Nevada was that of Joseph Walker in 1833 under the direction of Captain Benjamin Louis Eulalie de Bonneville.[11] Walker crossed the Great Salt Lake desert, moved southwest to the Humboldt, which he followed until it lost itself in the Humboldt sink. From here he set out across the Forty-mile desert to the Carson river, which led him to its source in the Sierra Nevada mountains. He came down from the mountains into the San Joaquin valley and went on to Monterey. On his return trip the following year, Walker was led by Indians to the pass through the Sierras south of Owen's lake which now bears his name. He turned north until he came upon the Walker river, which received his name from Fremont a decade later, and continued northward to the Carson river. Again he followed this stream to the Forty-mile desert and retraced his own route back to Utah.[12] This became the route of many of the emigrants and forty-niners; a large part of it, too, is the path followed by the first transcontinental railroad thirty-five years later.

Nevada beaver trapping was a short-lived enterprise. The trapping boom was declining nationally and the great basin was not a bounteous producer of beaver in any case. However, as the trappers were departing, the vanguard of the California-bound emigrants was advancing on the Great American desert. Many trappers turned scout, Joe Walker and Kit Carson perhaps the best remembered among them, to lead the emigrants through the basin country.

The first party of emigrants passed through Nevada in 1841. An amazingly ill-prepared group for the kind of trek which lay ahead of them, they somehow combined good fortune with plain courage and determination, and half a year after they pulled out of Independence, Missouri, wondering what direction they should be taking, they straggled into Dr. Marsh's farm at the foot of Mount Diablo in that land whose name sounded like magic to them, California.[13]

This was the John Bartleson party, named for its captain, although the real leader of group turned out to be young John Bidwell.[14] They had been lucky enough to meet an Oregon-bound party

[11] Mack, p. 70.

[12] Bancroft, pp. 41-45; Morgan, pp. 47-61.

[13] Morgan, p. 65.

[14] Five hundred persons had originally signed to make this trip, but John Bidwell was the only one of them who persevered in the intention. He gathered a new group of about seventy who actually left with him, and proved to be the strong man of the party in the trials that followed. Bartleson refused to go unless he was named captain. Some historians call it the Bidwell-Bartleson party. Cf. Morgan, p. 64.

led by the famous mountain man, Thomas Fitzpatrick. Still expecting to reach the legendary San Buenaventura, which would lead them across the Great Basin and guide them through the Sierra Nevadas to the land of their enchantment, they had even packed materials to make canoes when the time came. But before they left the Fitzpatrick group at Fort Hall, Idaho, they knew that a mean, mountainous desert lay between them and the mighty Sierra range which heralded California, and that their only hope in crossing the basin was in finding Mary's river (the Humboldt) with its shallow, bad-tasting alkaline waters. They had to abandon their wagons and learn to pack their horses and mules; they fought the elements and each other, stumbled and struggled and ate their mules to keep alive.[15] But somehow in the providence of God they made it to Dr. Marsh's and the emigrant trail to California—six months long—had been blazed. The first woman and child (Mrs. Benjamin Kelsey and her daughter, America) had crossed Nevada. Members of this party returned east and led other groups to California. Two years later the first wagon train, led by scout Joseph Walker, successfully made the trip by this new, shorter route to California through Nevada.[16]

It remained for Captain John Charles Fremont of the United States Army Topographical Engineers to put an end to the legend of the San Buenaventura and to write the reports and draw the maps of the Great Basin country, which became the regular handbooks of the future emigrants and added stimulus to westward travel.

Fremont first entered Nevada at its most northwestern corner in the winter of 1843, a French-styled howitzer his only wheeled carriage.[17] He travelled down the western edge of Nevada to Pyramid lake, followed the Truckee river (he called it the Salmon Trout river) for several miles before turning more southeasterly to the Carson and Walker rivers, and then he crossed the Sierras into California. Kit Carson and Thomas "Broken Hand" Fitzpatrick

[15] For details of this crossing, read Morgan, pp. 62-78.

[16] Mack, pp. 77-78.

[17] Fremont was commissioned to explore the continent of the Pacific Ocean for the United States. He was the son-in-law of Missouri Senator Thomas H. Benton, one of the spearheads of the expansionist drive in the senate, and was selected for the assignment through the senator's influence. He completed his task, reaching the Pacific in the Northwest and decided to take a southern route back, hoping to see Mary's river and to be the discoverer of the great San Buenaventura. The howitzer is of special interest to Nevadans because it was for many years the only souvenir in Nevada of the Fremont expeditions. The gun was kept at Virginia City and Glenbrook, until it disappeared in 1933. Cf. Mack, pp. 78, 82, and 93.

were his scouts, and Charles Preuss, a German scientist, served as his assistant in topography. Fremont expected at every mountain peak to look out upon a vista marked by the mythical Buenaventura, but discovered instead that what rivers he did find flowed east rather than west. In the Sierras he was finally forced, "to the great sorrow of the whole party," to abandon the howitzer, which he had dragged with him all the way from St. Louis and which had "commanded respect for us on some critical occasions."[18]

When Fremont returned east, after some weeks rest at Fort Sutter, he took the southern route, crossing the southern tip of Nevada, camping one night where Las Vegas is now situated. Fremont made his reports to the government, and sought to return to study the interior of the Great Basin more thoroughly, since he had actually only rimmed it. "The contents of the Great Basin are yet to be examined," he wrote in his *Memoirs*.[19]

Fremont returned to study central Nevada in 1845. Joe Walker was a scout on this expedition, as well as Carson and Fitzpatrick from the first one. Fremont broke the party into two groups. One section followed the Humboldt-Emigrant trail, and the other set out through the very middle of the basin (part of this route concurred with that of Jedediah Smith in 1827) with the two groups reassembling at Walker lake. Thus a topographical study of a vast portion of the Great Basin was accomplished in the one crossing.

Many of the names which Fremont gave to the rivers, lakes, and mountain passes have survived to this day. Walker river, Walker lake, Walker pass, Carson river, Pyramid lake, Humboldt river are among the more notable. With a nod to the Spanish priests of the 1776 maps, it must be said that John Charles Fremont really put Nevada on the map. His accurate reports were widely distributed in the East and few set out for California after that without first studying them or at least carrying them with them.[20]

The next three years saw the stream of California-bound emigrants crossing Nevada increase gradually. 1846 was the year of the ill-fated Donner party, more than half of whom lost their lives, when an early blizzard trapped them in the Sierras. Few stories of Ameri-

[18] Mack, p. 93, where she quotes Fremont, *Exploring Expedition*, p. 138.

[19] Mack, p. 97, where she quotes Fremont, *Memoirs*, pp. 391-392.

[20] The above account of the important Fremont expeditions is digested from the following detailed descriptions: Morgan, pp. 79-96; Mack, pp. 82-102; Bancroft, pp. 55-59; Thompson-West, pp. 24-25.

cana carry such horror, crudity, barbarism, and raw courage as is observed in the details of the crossing of this sad group, for whom the pass and lake in the Sierras, where the disaster occurred, have been named.[21]

The discovery of gold, January 24, 1848, on the South Fork of the American river, near Sacramento, California, turned this tiny stream of home seekers into a wild flood of gold seekers, the feverish forty-niners.[22] Across the Humboldt country they swept, wagon train on the heels of wagon train, an unfading cloud of dust marking the trail. Actually, they led to the settlement of Nevada, both directly and indirectly. The first settlements were begun in Nevada to cash in on the touring gold seekers. Nevada's first permanent settlers built supply stations for the booming tourist trade of their day. Their number was increased by the "tourists" themselves, some of whom moved back across the Sierras to Carson and Washoe valleys, when their dreams of California-gained wealth failed to materialize.

Two weeks after gold was discovered in California, that country, and along with it Nevada, Utah, and much of Arizona, New Mexico, Colorado, and Wyoming, became part of the United States. First this area had belonged to Spain. In 1821, it had come under Mexican control. The war between the States and Mexico was ended in February of 1848 with the treaty of Guadalupe Hidalgo, in which so much of the Far West was ceded to the United States.[23]

Nevada in 1849, and indeed through the fifties, was an unloved land. It was no more than a treacherous highway. Wagon ruts, a steadily rising stream of dust, a long, discouraging line of bones and graves and discarded belongings constituted the miserable memories recorded by the forty-niners. A count of the dead in 1850 revealed these figures: 1,061 dead mules, 4,960 dead horses, 3,750 dead oxen and cows, and 963 graves. Estimated value of abandonded property: one million dollars.[24]

Little wonder that at the end of this dreary, exhausting, costly trek across the Great Basin one would want to rest in the fertile valley along the Carson river before beginning the climb over the mighty Sierra Nevada mountains to California. Little wonder that

21 For the grim details of the Donner disaster, read Morgan, pp. 131-165.

22 Mack, p. 125.

23 *Loc. cit.*

24 *Ibid.*, p. 132.

the first supply station and permanent settlement in Nevada would be located in the Carson valley.

The first attempt to settle in Nevada occurred in 1850.[25] Hampden Beatie, member of a Mormon group on the way to the California goldfields, was struck by the beauty of Carson valley, and with a few companions left the gold seekers to start a trading post there. The group had great success, even erected a partial house (without roof or floor),[26] and that fall returned to Salt Lake City with glowing accounts of the place, although they lost their profit when Indians attacked and captured all their animals and supplies on their return to Salt Lake. The accounts of the Beatie party were augmented by others, leading to the permanent establishment of Mormon Station in 1851.[27]

The Mormons had arrived at the Great Salt Lake in 1847 and established their Zion there.[28] They organized the state of Deseret, including in their description of it most of what is now Nevada. At the same time organization of the new state of California was taking place. Some wished California to include Nevada and Utah country; others favored a smaller state, to stop on the east at the summit of the Sierra Nevadas. Congress settled the question on September 9, 1850, when it created the state of California, which was to be bounded on the east by the Sierras, and two new territories, New Mexico and Utah. Most of Nevada was included in the territory of Utah; a small portion of its southern tip was a part of the territory of New Mexico.[29]

Accordingly, it was for western Utah that John Reese and his party were bound in the spring of 1851.[30] They were heavily loaded

[25] Most historians have chosen 1849 for this event, However, Dale Morgan selects 1850 and offers the following logical explanation: "Nevada history, accepting the somewhat vague dates of H. S. Beatie in his manuscript, *The First in Nevada,* has always dated for 1849 the establishment of Mormon Station. Abner Blackburn's reliable reminiscences establish 1850 as correct. Beatie says that he came to Utah in C. T. Benson's company arriving here on the 26th of October, the year being assigned as 1848 from his saying subsequently that he arrived in Carson Valley in June, 1849. However, E. T. Benson did not come to Utah in 1848; he stayed in Iowa to oversee Mormon affairs with his co-apostles, George A. Smith and Orson Hyde. He led to Utah a large company of the Mormon immigration of 1849, arriving in Salt Lake Valley October 28th. Beatie's information was given from memory of 1884." Morgan, pp. 199-200.

[26] Mack, p. 147.

[27] *Ibid.,* p. 148.

[28] This migration is described in Morgan, pp. 166-179.

[29] Mack, pp. 145-146.

[30] *Ibid.,* p. 149.

with supplies to start a trading post in that fertile valley beyond the Forty-mile desert, about which they had heard such good reports. On July 4 they arrived at the Beatie place, which Reese bought from two people. He gave a man named Moore about twenty dollars (Moore is thought to have bought the place from Beatie) and paid Captain Jim, a Washoe Indian, two sacks of flour for the land. During the summer Reese completed the building, fenced off some thirty acres which he had claimed, planted a large turnip crop to sell to the oncoming forty-niners. As the summer wore on, he was joined by other Mormons, by some miners who came over from Placer county, California, and by several California-bound travelers, who arrived in the fall and decided to spend the winter at Mormon Station rather than risk the dangerous, snowy, mountain trip into California. Thus was established the first permanent settlement in Nevada.[31]

Mormon Station was very much its own place. After all, it was separated from California both by law and by a more imposing barrier, the Sierra Nevadas. Also, it was some eight hundred miles removed from Salt Lake City by the Humboldt trail, which took about a month of travel.[32] As an outpost of Zion it was hardly a success. Brigham Young was able to exercise little or no influence, either as governor of the territory of Utah or as head of the Morman Church. These first Nevada settlers were an independent group. By the time a man got to Mormon Station and settled down, he ought to feel free and independent, and very much "on his own." God knows he was.

On November 12, 1851, "the citizens of Western Utah" held their first meeting. There were maybe a hundred settlers in the area at the time. They wanted law and order, and they knew where to look for it: from themselves and eventually from Congress. Accordingly, they specified at this meeting that it was their intention: 1) to adopt a system of rules through which the settlers could subdivide "the valley so as to secure each individual in their rights to land taken up and improved by them;" 2) to petition Congress for a distinct territorial government; 3) to create public offices for the valley; 4) to adopt bylaws and fixed regulations to govern the community. They provided for a survey of land claims, limited claims to quarter sections, created the offices of recorder and treasurer,

[31] *Ibid.*, pp. 149-150; Thompson-West, p. 31.

[32] Mormon Station was 853 miles from Salt Lake by the Humboldt trail. Later the mail route was 689 miles, and Simpson's route was 565. Cf. Morgan, p. 233.

elected a seven-man committee to serve as the executive department, and drafted their petition to Congress.[33]

One week later the group met for the second time and again property laws were foremost in their minds. They gave parties the right to take a new claim, after they had disposed of the one in possession. They required that a twenty-five dollar prepayment fee be made to the recorder, and that a claimant put a minimum of five dollars into improvements on his land within 180 days after receiving his certificate.[34] They permitted a company to take claims for each member of the company and to improve one location enough for all. They declared that timber land was common property, making an exception for persons erecting a saw mill, to whom they allotted an unspecified number of acres.[35] Thus the first effective property laws in Nevada were passed, with fine disregard for the actual, though unenforceable, law of the land, the laws of the territory of Utah.

The group was not finished with its organization of a squatter government. They assembled again the following day and created the offices of justice of the peace, clerk of the court, and sheriff "to exercise and enforce law according to the acknowledged rules of equity which govern all civilized communities." The justice of the peace was given the power to summon any four persons on a given occasion to form with him a court of law "to take cognizance and adjudicate summarily in all cases of controversy, debts or offenses against the public weal; and to enforce fines or other sufficient penalties upon offenders; to issue warrants and authorize arrests." A defendent had the right of appeal from the decisions of this court to a court of twelve citizens, "summoned promiscuously." This latter court could reverse the former decision, and remove or fine the

[33] Records of this and the subsequent meetings of these first settlers were kept in a small, sixty-page book which has been preserved. Thompson-West quotes extensively from this original document and therefore has served as the main source of the above and immediately following paragraphs. Cf. Thompson-West, pp. 32-34.

[34] This rule was amended March 21, 1853, at the fifth meeting of the residents. The amendment stipulated that no one could hold land, until they had filed a notice of claim for it with the recorder. They had to put one hundred dollars in improvements into the land within sixty days after filing the claim. Occupancy by the principal or his agent was made necessary to title. It was further ruled at this meeting that a family man could claim 640 acres, a single person 320 acres. The fee to be paid to the recorder was reduced to five dollars. Cf. Thompson-West, pp. 32-34.

[35] At the fourth meeting of the group, May 22, 1852, it was determined that anyone building a saw mill could take a full section of timber land. Cf. Thompson-West, p. 32.

magistrate for abuses of his office. From this court there was no further appeal.[36]

Before they adjourned, the citizens elected their first justice, clerk and sheriff, and squatter government in Nevada was in force. It was just eight days since their first meeting. It was hardly more than four months since John Reese had ridden into the area and started this first Nevada settlement.

Mormon Station was surely a sore spot to the government in Salt Lake City. One of the brothers reported to Brigham Young in 1852 that the Carson valley residents:

> declare in language too strong to utter that they will no longer be governed or tried by Mormon laws, that they are chiefly organized here to redress the wrongs inflicted on United States citizens who had the good luck, or were fortunate enough to escape with life and limb from Utah . . . Col. Reese and his nephew Mr. Kinsey who are both so good and accomodating while in Salt Lake have been the ringleaders in opposing the organization of the territory of Utah and declare they will pay no taxes what are levied on them from that source and advise others to hold out in like manner until they get this valley annexed to California.[37]

The Saints at Zion became further worried about their brothers in Carson valley, as more reports of this nature were made about them. " . . . And as to Mormonism," wrote one, "I can't find it here."[38] A number of Mormons were, therefore, "called" to move to the Carson valley outpost to strengthen their brothers there in numbers, and no doubt in faith also. But at the same time, more and more miners were drifting back over the Sierras to the eastern valleys to prospect the hills on that side. A growing Mormon-Gentile split was festering in the valley, and the desire for annexation to California was being strengthened with the growth of the gentile population.[39]

An effort to stop this tide away from Utah was made on January 17, 1854, when the Utah legislature created the county of Carson

[36] *Loc. cit.*

[37] Morgan, pp. 203-204.

[38] *Loc. cit.*

[39] *Ibid.*, p. 205.

and authorized the governor to name a probate judge to organize it. This legislature also divided Utah into three judicial districts, one of which was the newly created Carson county. The governor named Orson Hyde, a Morman elder, as probate judge of the new county at the far western limits of Utah. Judge Hyde and his party arrived at Mormon Station June 15, 1855, and immediately set about organizing county government. An election for county officers was held, September 20, 1855, and all officers elected but one, the prosecuting attorney, were Mormons. This result was not accepted mildly by the gentiles, and Judge Hyde discovered that it was not going to be easy to bring Utah law to this valley, where too many preferred their old squatter government to what they considered an outside-imposed one from Salt Lake City.[40]

Judge Hyde had Mormon Station surveyed and changed its name to Genoa, for reasons which have not survived although the name has.[41] He laid out Franktown in Washoe valley, where he himself settled and started a saw mill. More and more Mormons moved into the area, taking over the agricultural lands of Carson, Jack's, Eagle, and Washoe valleys. Their political supremacy increased, and so, proportionately, did the unrest of the gentiles.[42]

A Mormon-Gentile War might well have developed (one was threatened for a couple of weeks but called off when the gentiles sent to Placer, California, for assistance) had it not been for a greater war intervening.[43] The Mormons were becoming a seriously disturbing group to the federal government. Their disputes with the California-bound emigrants, their practice of polygamy, their quarreling with and "open defiance" of the United States officers in the territory led to the Utah War of 1857.[44] President Buchanan sent a division of the United States Army, under General A. Sydney Johnston, to quiet the "rebellious" Mormons and restore the supremacy of the federal government in Utah. Brigham Young called for all Mormons everywhere to return to the City of the Saints to assist in its defense against the "armed mob of Gentiles."[45]

40 Mack, pp. 154-157.

41 Mack, however, writes that Genoa was chosen in honor of the birthplace of Columbus. This is a reasonable surmise in view of the fact that these same residents later wanted to have the territory named for Columbus. Cf. Mack, p. 158; *Infra*, p. 13.

42 *Ibid.*, p. 159.

43 *Ibid.*, p. 165.

44 *Ibid.*, pp. 167-168.

45 Thompson-West, p. 41.

Peace was restored April 6, 1858, after a conference between Brigham Young and Colonel Thomas L. Kane, who had befriended the Mormons at Nauvoo, Illinois, in 1846, and therefore was best qualified to engineer peaceful terms with them on behalf of the federal government.[46]

However, the Utah War brought an end to Mormon supremacy in Western Utah. The great majority of the Mormons had obediently answered Brigham Young's call and left their farms in the Carson valley area, selling them "for a trifle" in their haste to return to Salt Lake City. Some returned after the war, but their numerical majority was gone. Western Utah had been taken over by the gentiles.[47]

There was little semblance of government in these valleys after the Mormons left in 1857, until the territory of Nevada was created in 1861. There were at times three would-be governments trying to exist at once, but the general effect was confusion and lawlessness. However, the tenor of the people was clear. They wanted their own government; they would no longer countenance rule from Eastern Utah.

While the Mormons were still packing to leave the Carson valley region in 1857, the gentiles (and some apostate Mormons who had decided to stay behind) were assembling in Genoa to ready a new petition to Congress for separate territorial government. As the boundaries of new territory, they named fairly exactly the present limits of the state of Nevada. They selected Genoa for the capital and asked that the new territory be named "Columbus." James M. Crane was chosen as delegate in Washington.[48]

Crane nearly succeeded in having the new territory created by Congress in 1858. The bill passed the lower house and had reached the third reading in the senate, when Senator Gwin of California, in whose hands he had entrusted it, dropped it as interfering with his Arizona bill. The committee which had studied the bill had left it intact with one exception: they had changed the name of the proposed territory from "Columbus" to "Nevada."[49]

Meanwhile, the residents at home were trying to form a new squatters government of their own. The people's tribunal which re-

46 Mack, p. 169.
47 *Ibid.*, pp. 169-172
48 *Ibid.*, pp. 174-175.
49 *Ibid.*, p. 176.

sulted was a capricious group at best, some of whose acts of justice are as questionable as the crimes they purported to avenge.[50] At the same time, the Utah authorities were attempting to reorganize Carson county under new probate judge, John S. Childs. An election in October only added to the confusion and general unrest. Votes of whole precincts were discarded as illegal and those elected were ignored or refused to take office.[51] In June of 1859 another attempt at territorial government was made. This time the residents voted to draw up a constitution, send a delegate to Congress once more, and elect a slate of "state" officers. James Crane was again named delegate to Congress, and Issac Roop was elected governor of the provisional government. Crane died that fall, and John J. Musser was selected to replace him. Musser went to Washington, but found the thirty-fifth Congress too concerned with other matters, such as the approaching presidential election, to consider the bill for the territory of Nevada.[52]

Isaac Roop made some sallies towards the organization of the people's provisional government. Probate Judge Childs held another election, in which very few turned out to vote and none of those elected would take office. Thirdly, the federal government arrived on the scene in the person of Judge John Cradlebaugh, a United States district judge. It was thought that he might have some control because of a popularity in the area stemming from his attempts to bring some of the Mormons there to trial in regard to the Mountain Meadows massacre. Thus in 1859 three governments were trying to function in the area, but as a matter of fact everyone was doing generally as he pleased.[53]

That summer a great influx of miners stormed into the area after discovery of the rich Comstock lode in June. Virginia City, Gold Hill, Nevada City (Dayton) were beginning to be the centers of the area's quickly growing population. The great silver strike was changing the nature of the place from farm and trading post to boisterous mining camp. Carson City had been laid out in the fall of 1858 and was the new center of governmental efforts, probably because it was centrally located in Eagle valley, with Carson valley

[50] *Ibid.*, p. 177. For details of some of the more famous "incidents" of this people's tribunal, read Morgan's interesting chapter, which he has aptly entitled "Variations on the Theme of Murder." Morgan, pp. 208-221.

[51] Mack, p. 178.

[52] *Ibid.*, pp. 180-184

[53] *Loc. cit.*

and Genoa on one side, Washoe valley and Franktown on another, and Mount Davidson with its mining camps on a third.[54]

Two vigorous lawyers appeared on the scene in 1860. William Stewart was a Yale graduate and an outspoken unionist. David Terry was a southerner, sent some said, by Jefferson Davis to see that the proposed new territory became a part of the Southern Confederacy. Each was a good lawyer; big men, outspoken, firm, they were natural protagonists. In June, 1860, they agreed to try their cases before United States district judge, John Cradlebaugh. Thus some semblance of governmental control was exerted.[55]

However, in October of that year President Buchanan appointed a new district judge, R. P. Fleniken, and a new dispute was in full swing. Stewart supported Cradlebaugh in his claim that Buchanan's appointment was illegal. Terry supported Fleniken. Once again little judicial work could be done effectively. When the supreme court of the territory of Utah upheld a Cradlebaugh decision in a test case, Fleniken accepted his competency, although some physical persuasion was also required.[56] With the outbreak of the Civil War Terry left, but Stewart and Cradlebaugh remained.[57] Cradlebaugh then represented the only effectual authority in the area until the territory was created in 1861.

Into this scene of lawless confusion rode the first priests to pioneer the establishment of the Catholic Church in Nevada. Before Nevada became a part of the United States in 1850, it was a part of the diocese of Sonora, Mexico, and later the diocese of the two Californias under Bishop Garcia Diego y Moreno. When this region was ceded to the United States in 1850, the Church, following national lines, removed its ecclesiastical jurisdiction from Mexico, and established the diocese of Monterey as a part of the American diocesan system. Nevada was a part of that diocese. In 1853 the archdiocese of San Francisco was created, and Nevada was included in the territory assigned to the new archdiocese. Up to this time no missionary activity had been carried on by the Church in the "Unknown Land" or

[54] Cf. Morgan, pp. 248-268, for details on the discovery of silver. There had been some mining in Nevada since 1850, but on a small scale until the silver discovery.

[55] Mack, pp. 186-188.

[56] *Ibid.*, pp. 188-189.

[57] Stewart became one of the greatest figures in the political history of Nevada. He was the principal framer of the Nevada Constitution, was one of Nevada's first senators, serving in the upper house from 1865 to 1875 and again from 1887 to 1905. His home in Carson City is the present rectory of St. Theresa's church there.

among the few Mormon settlers who had established the first trading posts and farms in the Carson Valley.[58]

However, with the rising influx of miners from California to the hills on the eastern side of the Sierras, Archbishop Sadoc Alemany of San Francisco named Father Joseph Gallagher pastor of Genoa, Carson, and Virginia in 1858. No records have been found of Father Gallagher's administrations and so it is not known where the first Mass in Nevada was offered.[59] However, it may be safely assumed that the pioneer priest visited throughout the area: at Genoa, which was probably still the largest settlement that year; at Carson, which was just being laid out; at Franktown and Johntown, Gold Hill, Virginia, and Chinatown (or Mineral Rapids, as its white inhabitants then preferred to call the place which was finally named Dayton).[60]

Two years later, in August of 1860, Father Hugh Gallagher, Joseph Gallagher's brother, came to the area. The second Father Gallagher built three small churches, one at Genoa, one at Carson City, and one at Virginia City.[61] There was virtually no government in the country; miners were streaming in to lay claims and fight for them against all contenders. Stewart and Terry were arguing some mining claims before Judge Cradlebaugh. In the midst of such legal and governmental confusion, one can well surmise that the priest merely staked his claim like everybody else or bought the land from an individual without benefit of a county recorder. It is questionable how anyone's title to property was held that year, and certainly the Church's title would be no exception.

At any rate, Father Gallagher had a sorry time of it with his three little churches. The one in Genoa was seized by creditors and for many years was that community's court house. The one in Carson was blown down by a Washoe zephyr and a similar winter storm destroyed Virginia City's little church, too.[62]

Father Hugh Gallagher's stay in Nevada was a brief one, as had been his brother's before him. The vicariate of Marysville was

[58] Cf. Gorman, *Seventy-Five Years of Catholic Life in Nevada* (Reno: Journal Press, 1935), p. 9 (hereafter cited Gorman). Bishop Gorman compiled this work from original sources shortly after he came to Nevada as first Bishop of Reno in 1931.

[59] Gorman, p. 41.

[60] Dayton was also called Nevada City and Hall's Station. Cf. Mack, p. 160.

[61] Gorman, pp. 41-42 and 60.

[62] *Ibid.*, p. 60.

created in 1860, including in its boundaries all of Nevada north of the thirty-ninth degree of latitude. Southern Nevada, south of the thirty-ninth parallel, remained part of the archdiocese of San Francisco.[63] Since Father Gallagher's parish was in the new vicariate, he returned to San Francisco where he became the first pastor of St. Joseph's parish, a post he held until his death in 1882.[64]

Responding to numerous pleas from the residents of the Carson valley area, the two California sentors, Gwin and Latham, took up the cause of a Nevada territory in Washington. President Buchanan signed the bill creating the territory of Nevada on March 2, 1861, one of his last acts as president.[65] His successor, President Lincoln, named James W. Nye, a New York Whig Democrat, governor of the new territory. He arrived in July and declared the organization of the territorial government on July 11. An election was held in August and at last a valid, operative, legal history of Nevada could begin.[66]

The next two years were filled with the establishment of county governments, judicial districts, a legal code (the California and New York codes were the models),[67] and the settlement of a dispute with California over the western boundary line of the new territory.[68]

Almost immediately agitation for statehood began. At the first territorial legislature it was determined to submit the question of statehood to the voters. This was done and the sentiment was overwhelmingly in favor of statehood. In 1863 Congress passed an enabling act for the state of Nevada. Accordingly, that fall a constitutional convention assembled in Carson City and framed a constitution. The voters, however, turned down this first constitution at the polls. They were opposed to the mining tax and to a provision that the various offices created by the constitution should be filled at the same time the vote on the constitution iself was taken.[69] These two provisions were corrected in the second constitution which was

[63] *Ibid.*, p. 10.

[64] *Ibid.*, p. 60.

[65] Mack. p. 161.

[66] For details of the organization of the territory, see Mack, pp 218-228.

[67] *Ibid.*, pp. 229-245.

[68] A thorough review of this boundary dispute may be found in Mack's chapter, "Geographical Evolution of Nevada," pp. 381-409.

[69] *Ibid.*, pp. 249-253.

[70] *Ibid.*, p. 257.

offered to the voters the following year, and this time the voters accepted it by a wide majority.[70]

Agitation for Nevada statehood within the territory itself came mostly from the mining element. Corruption among the district judges and an inadequate national mining code left the mining claims in a very uncertain state. The miners were convinced that security in their mine holdings would only come with statehood.[71] But the greater and more effective agitation for Nevada statehood was taking place in Washington itself, in the White House. President Lincoln asked congress to encourage immigration to Nevada, since the parcity of its population was the biggest obstacle to its statehood, and spoke of the early possibility of organizing it as a state. The president was looking forward to the three votes from Nevada, which he was assured would be cast in favor of his emancipation proclamation and which would be enough to carry it. Indeed, when New York and New Jersey opposed Nevada statehood, Lincoln instructed Secretary Charles Dana to give them whatever they wanted to influence them to change their vote on Nevada. "Here is the alternative:" he said, "that we carry this vote, or be compelled to raise another million, and I don't know how many more men, and fight no one knows how long. It is a question of three votes or new armies."[72]

Dana was successful, and Nevada became a state October 31, 1864. However, it was not until the following February that its senators arrived in Washington. The same day that Nevada's representatives took their seats in Congress, the thirteenth amendment was passed, and sixteen days later the new state of Nevada ratified it. Small as the new state was, population-wise, it had cast a gigantic vote for the federal government.[73]

While the territory of Nevada was taking these steps towards statehood in the early sixties, the Catholic Church was also making the first strides towards its establishment there. The genuine foundations of the Church in Nevada were laid by Father Patrick Manogue, who arrived in Virginia City in late June, 1862. The brief visits of the two brothers, Fathers Joseph and Hugh Gallagher, in 1858 and 1860, had been followed by another short stay, that of

[71] *Ibid.*, pp. 253-254, and 258-264.
[72] *Ibid.*, p. 256.
[73] *Ibid.*, p. 266.

Father C. Delahunty in 1861.[74] None of these first three pastors to administer the Sacraments in Nevada remained in the area long enough to establish a permanent base for the Catholic development of the territory. Father Manogue did that.

Bishop O'Connell, who became Vicar Apostolic of Marysville when that vicariate was named in 1860, created the parish of Virginia City in 1862. The new parish included all of Nevada north of the thirty-ninth parallel.[75] As first pastor of the new, and territorially very extensive, parish, Bishop O'Connell chose a newly ordained priest: healthy, vigorous, well-acquainted with the miners, 41 year-old Patrick Manogue. This energetic Irishman had come to the United States when he was 17, lived in Connecticut for a time, studied at St. Mary's of the Lake college in Chicago for four years, then mined at Moore's Flats, California, near Nevada City, for three more years. With his savings from the mines he traveled to Paris, where he studied philosophy and theology at the seminary of St. Sulpice and was ordained a priest in 1861. The young priest returned west and for his first assignment was selected to begin the new parish in the booming mining camp, Virginia City.[76]

Immediately upon his arrival in Virginia City towards the end of June (his first entry in the parish records is dated July 1, 1862), Father Manogue went to work to build a church to replace the little one Father Gallagher had built there two years earlier only to have it blown down. The new church, a frame structure, was dedicated to St. Mary in the Mountains. It soon became too small for Father Manogue's growing congregation and was replaced in 1868 by a large, brick church, which was an "ornament to the city." In 1875, Father Manogue gave permission to dynamite this fine edifice in order to prevent the spreading of the great fire which destroyed a large section of the city. Two years later he had replaced it with the stately, Gothic building, which today still towers as the principal landmark of this famous old mining camp.[77]

Two years after his arrival in Virginia City, Father Manogue opened the first Catholic schools and orphanage in Nevada. The Sisters of Charity of St. Vincent de Paul from San Francisco staffed

[74] Gorman, p. 41.
[75] *Ibid.*, p. 42.
[76] *Ibid.*, p. 20.
[77] *Ibid.*, p. 43.

a school for girls, a school for small boys, and the orphanage, all of which were housed in one building constructed for the combined purposes. Father Manogue next built a hospital in his parish, which was opened in 1876 and also conducted by the Sisters of Charity. The orphanage and hospital were not only the first such Catholic institutions in Nevada, but the first orphanage and hospital to be built by anyone in that area.[78]

How title was held to these first Catholic properties is a question which may never be fully answered. The loss of records through fire has left insoluble doubts about many of these problems of early Nevada. The only information able to be discovered about the Virginia City properties is a statement in the Virginita City Directory of 1878-1879, stating the location of the church, listing Father Manogue as pastor and Father P. McGuire as assistant, and numbering the members of the parish at 4,000. The hospital and schools are also named and located in the directory, where it is stated that the ground upon which the hospital is located was a gift of Mrs. J. W. Mackey to the Sisters of Charity. The 1886 Book of Deeds for Ormsby County records that the Catholic church in Carson City was deeded to the Right Rev. Eugene O'Connell, who was Bishop of Maryville. A deed, dated October 4, 1875, in Douglas County names J. S. Allemany, Archbishop of San Francisco and Ex-Officio Trustee of Catholic Church property, as the one holding title to the church in Genoa. These are the earliest records of the manner of holding church property in Nevada which have so far come to light.[79]

St. Mary in the Mountains is the mother parish of Nevada. The first parishes to be cut off from it, as Mount Davidson mining flourished, were Divide and Gold Hill in 1863. Other parishes, formed directly from the Virginia City parish in the early days of the Church in Nevada, include: Austin, 1864; Carson City, 1865; Hamilton, 1869; Reno, 1871; Eureka, 1872.[80]

Virginia City's first pastor was also its longest and most active, since he was there during the mining camp's most prosperous days. In 1881 he was named coadjutor bishop to Bishop O'Connell of

[78] *Ibid.*, pp. 45-47.

[79] This information was received by the writer in a letter from Harley W. Carter, Manager of the Nevada Title Guaranty Company, Carson City Branch.

[80] Gorman, p. 42.

Grass Valley.[81] The diocese of Grass Valley had been created in 1868 to replace the vicariate of Marysville.[82] Bishop Manogue succeeded to the Grass Valley see in 1884, and two years later he became the first bishop of Sacramento, when the see was moved to California's capital city from the declining mining town. Bishop Manogue continued to display the building genius which had marked his nineteen, industrious years in Virginia City. The beautiful Cathedral of the Blessed Sacrament in Sacramento, completed and dedicated in 1889, is his work. This great pioneer miner, priest, and bishop of the Far West died February 27, 1895.[83] Nevada's first Catholic high school, opened in Reno in 1948, was named for him.

That part of Nevada below the thirty-ninth parallel remained under the jursidiction of the archdiocese of San Francisco until 1887. At that time Utah and southern and eastern Nevada were placed under the jurisdiction of the newly created vicariate apostolic of Utah. Four years later this Vicariate was erected into the diocese of Salt Lake.[84] Vicar apostolic of Utah and later first bishop of Salt Lake was another early pioneer priest who left his mark upon Nevada, Bishop Lawrence Scanlon. Father Scanlon, a priest of the Cathedral staff in San Francisco, just 27 years old and two years ordained, responded to a request from Bishop Alemany for a priest to go to Pioche, at the eastern edge of Nevada, to establish the Church there. The young priest built a church in Pioche and also administered the sacraments throughout southeastern Nevada. He remained only three years before returning to California, but a short time later he volunteered again, this time to go to Utah. Father Scanlon became the great pioneer priest of Salt Lake, where be built churches, schools, hospitals, brought in the Sisters of the Holy Cross. He became vicar apostolic in 1887 and bishop of Salt Lake in 1891. From then until his death in 1915, he governed Utah and a great portion or Nevada, namely, the counties of Elko, White Pine, Eureka, Lander, Lincoln, Nye and Clark.[85]

An important factor in determining the location of many of the communities which sprang up in the early years of the state of Nevada was the railroad. The fertile valleys at the foot of the Sierra

[81] *Ibid.*, p. 20.
[82] *Ibid.*, p. 11.
[83] *Ibid.*, pp. 20-21.
[84] *Ibid.*, p. 12.
[85] *Ibid.*, pp. 21-23.

Nevadas attracted the first settlements. The discovery of gold and silver caused the sudden mushrooming of the mining camps throughout the great basin country, and the running out of those ore veins saw just as sudden a decline of those camps into the ghost towns of today. In the sixties, however, the Central Pacific Railroad Company raced through Nevada, laying a new, steel trail across the Great Basin. The Union Pacific was coming from the East, and the two companies were bidding for the Salt Lake rights, which would be awarded to the one which arrived there first.[86] Stations along the path of the new railroad grew into some of Nevada's most vigorous communities and outlived many of the more glamorous mining camps. Reno sprang suddenly into existence when the first through-train arrived at its site from Sacramento on June 18, 1868. It made a junction with the railroad to Virginia City, was located next to the Truckee river in a fertile valley, altogether an attractice place to live. More than two hundred lots were sold the first day, causing it to be described as a "mushroom town which sprang up overnight."[87] It quickly grew, soon becoming the largest city in the state, until Nevada's most recent boom town, Las Vegas, also a railroad station at the start, shot past it in population after the Second World War.

The Central Pacific Railroad won its hectic race with the Union Pacific. The two companies joined their tracks (with a Comstock silver spike) at Promontory Point, Utah, May 10, 1869.[88] The railroad reached from the Atlantic to the Pacific at last. The wagon trails could become obsolete now, as a new era in the nation's growth was beginning. Along the railroad, much of which followed the Humboldt trail, grew the towns of Wells, Elko, Carlin, Battle Mountain, Winnemucca, Lovelock, Sparks, and Reno.[89] Missions and parishes were quickly begun in these new communities by the Church. Offshoots of the mining camp parishes, these are the ones which survive today—long after many of the mother parishes have been suppressed with the decline of Nevada mining—and are the centers of much of the Catholic life of Nevada today.

On March 27, 1931, Pope Pius XI created the diocese of Reno. The new diocese comprised the whole state of Nevada, part of it

[86] Cf. Morgan, pp. 288-303, for the story of this famous race and the laying of the railroad through Nevada.

[87] Mack, p. 379.

[88] Morgan, p. 302.

[89] *Ibid.*, 305.

being taken from the diocese of Sacramento and part of it from the diocese of Salt Lake. Thomas K. Gorman, a priest of the archdiocese of Los Angeles, was named its first bishop. Consecrated July 22, the new bishop arrived in Reno and took canonical possession of his see on August 18, 1931. An herculean task faced the enterprising young bishop (he was not quite 39), who had to establish a self-sufficient diocese and was beginning with just thirteen priests, scattered over 110,829 square miles in eleven parishes.[90]

Bishop Gorman, truly a modern pioneer, remained in Nevada for twenty-one years, creating new parishes, building schools and hospitals, introducing new groups of sisters and catechists, quadrupling his clergy, stimulating Catholic activity among the laity. He is now bishop of the diocese of Dallas-Fort Worth, Texas.[91]

Bishop Gorman was succeeded in Reno by Bishop Robert J. Dwyer. Bishop Dwyer was a priest of the diocese of Salt Lake City, where he was consecrated August 5, 1952. He took canonical possession of the diocese of Reno, August 19, 1952, and is currently serving as the young diocese's second bishop.

Most recent years in Nevada, as in all the West, have seen a tremendous population growth, especially in its two largest cities, Las Vegas and Reno. A new century's forty-niners are rushing into these lands from the East, creating new boom towns. The Church, under Bishop Dwyer's astute leadership, has had to keep pace with the sudden, post-war influx by creating new parishes, building schools, increasing the clergy and sisterhood in the diocese. In many ways it would appear that what has been written here of the early struggles of Nevada is not so much its history as a mere preface to its true chronicle, the events of which are yet to take place.

90 Gorman, p. 35.

91 Cf. *Nevada Register,* September 14, 1956. A special edition, commemorating the twenty-fifth anniversary of the diocese of Reno, lists the major Catholic works and achievements during the twenty-one years of Bishops Gorman's administration and the first four years of that of his successor, Bishop Dwyer.

CHAPTER II

NEVADA CORPORATION LAWS

Nevada jurisprudence defines a corporation as "an artificial person, a distinct legal entity, and its officers are its agents."[1] The civil law creates corportions in order that groups of persons or institutions may hold property and perform legal acts just as a natural person does. Thus the state gives societies, associations, companies, churches, hospitals, schools, etc., an artificial personality. This artificial person, a legal entity created by the state, is endowed with certain powers by which it acts for the whole group or for the institution.

Where Nevada jurisprudence speaks of artificial personality, canon law uses the term moral personality. The civil law speaks of corporations; canon law describes moral persons. The Code[2] divides moral persons into two classes, collegiate and non-collegiate.[3] A collegiate moral person is constituted by a number of physical persons, not less than three.[4] It is a legal entity, distinct from the individuals who are its members, having rights and obligations independent of its members. A non-collegiate moral person consists of property or goods, rather than persons, such as a hospital or seminary. Both collegiate and non-collegiate moral persons in the Church must be dedicated to some religious or charitable purpose.[5]

The Catholic Church and the Apostolic See have the nature of a moral person by divine institution.[6] Christ founded the Church as a perfect society: supreme, autonomous, independent, having within itself all the means necessary to fulfill its supernatural end. To exercise these means it must have the status of moral personality. Therefore, it is from divine foundation, rather than from any civil endowment, that the Church and the Apostolic See are moral persons.[7] Here is a departure from the concept of civil law. American

[1] Ex parte Rickey, 100 P. 134 (1909), 31 Nev. 82, 135 Am. St. Rep. 651.

[2] The term *Code* in this work will refer solely to the Code of Canon Law, *Codex Iuris Canonici, Pii X Pontificis Maximi iussu digestus, Benedicti Papae XV auctoritate promulgatus* (Romae: Typis Polglottis Vaticanis, 1917).

[3] Canon 99. "Canon" in Church law is similar to "statute" in civil law.

[4] Canon 100,§2.

[5] Canon 100,§1.

[6] *Loc. cit.*

[7] "The distinction between these two moral persons is a *real, inadequate distinction;* one is part of the other. The Apostolic See, in this connection, does *not* in-

jurisprudence recognizes only one type of moral personality, the corporation. A corporation, and accordingly a moral person, cannot exist without the approval of the proper civil authority. Thus, American law maintains that the state gives the Church moral personality, but canon law holds that Christ gave the Church moral personality when He founded it as a perfect society.[8] Recognizing this difference in thinking, the Church protects its divine rights by incorporating its subordinate moral persons according to the statutes of the various States and has experienced little difficulty in the matter, rather enjoying the opportunity to develop its various religious and charitable institutions with great freedom.[9]

Only the Church as such and the Apostolic See are moral persons by divine institution. Inferior moral persons in the Church receive their moral personality from ecclesiastical authority, either by provision of the law itself or by a formal decree of the proper ecclesiastical authority.[10] The College of Cardinals and the diocesan Curia have received their moral personality by provision of the law.[11] New dioceses are created as moral persons by formal decree of the Holy See, and new parishes by the decree of the bishop.[12]

Since Nevada was made a territory in 1861, its legislatures have passed several laws through which corporations may be formed in Nevada. Some of those acts are of such a nature that the various Catholic institutions and societies may incorporate under them. Although none of the corporation laws of Nevada expressly forbid churches or religious societies from incorporating under them, their very nature would for the most part exclude such action. However, before examining the particular laws which are most applicable to the needs of the Church in Nevada, it would be well to review briefly all the major corporation legislation. The articles which follow will summarize the legislative history of Nevada corporation law, the pro-

clude the departments of the Roman Curia (cf. c.7). Bouscaren-Ellis, *Canon Law* (Milwaukee: Bruce, 1951), pp. 86-87 (hereafter cited Bouscaren).

[8] Cf. Murphy, *The Laws of the State of New York Affecting Church Property,* The Catholic University of American Canon Law Studies, n. 388 (Washington, D.C.: The Catholic University of America Press, 1957), pp. 16-17 (hereafter cited Murphy); *infra,* pp. 48, 50.

[9] Woywod, *A Practical Commentary on the Code of Canon Law* (revised by Callistus Smith, revised and enlarged edition, 2 Vols., New York: Jos. F. Wagner, Inc. 1948) I, 54-55 (hereafter cited Woywod).

[10] Canon 100,§1.

[11] Canons 231, 241, 363.

[12] Canons 248,§2 and 216,§1.

cedure required for the formation of the principal types of corporations presently in force in Nevada law, the powers of those corporations, and the rules for their dissolution.

ARTICLE 1. LEGISLATIVE HISTORY OF NEVADA CORPORATIONS

Nevada's second territorial legislature in 1862 passed two corporation laws. The first, approved December 19, was entitled "An Act to provide for the incorporation of religious, charitable, literary, scientific, and other association,"[13] and outlined the steps for the formation of these corporations, listed their powers and the method required for their dissolution. The second, approved the following day, was a more general corporation law, intended, apparently, to cover all other types of groups which might wish to incorporate in the territory. It was called "An Act to provide for the formation of corporations for certain purposes." An enactment, "amendatory and supplementary to" this latter act, was approved by the last territorial legislature, February 19, 1864.[14]

Nevada became a state on October 31, 1864, and convened its first state legislature the following year. The legislature of 1865 approved four separate corporation laws. "An Act to authorize the incorporation of rural cemetery associations" was approved March 1, 1865. This law is still on the Nevada books, unchanged from its original form, as no amendments have ever been made to it. The act lays down the procedure necessary to form such associations, the powers of the corporations, its right to land and the limitation thereto, rules for the election of trustees, their rights and duties, and contains as well several sections treating injury, bequeaths, tax exemption, the inalienability of individual lots, and the rights of lot owners.[15]

On March 10, 1865, legislators approved a new "Act to provide for the formation of corporations for certain purposes."[16] This law contained a repealer, through which the act approved under the same title by the territorial legislature of 1862 and the amendatory and supplementary act of 1864 were both repealed. The new act was more general than the first two, being framed in language of such a nature as to allow more types of corporations to be formed under it.

[13] B. 333. Cf. p. 141, for an explanation of this and succeeding abbreviations.
[14] C. 892.
[15] BH. 1045.
[16] BH. 805.

"An Act to provide for the organization and maintenance of historic, scientific, and other literary societies" was approved March 20, 1865.[17] This act did not repeal the somewhat similar law of 1862. It eliminated religious and charitable associations and added historic. Hence, while it partially overlaps the earliest act, it cannot be said to supersede it entirely.

The fourth corporation law passed by this first state legislature was a special act "to provide for the incorporation of railroads," approved March 22, 1865.[18] The first transcontinental railroad was being talked about in great earnestness in those days and was completed just four years after this corporation act was approved in Nevada.

Nevada's second state legislature approved two more corporation laws. A new act "to provide for the incorporation of religious, charitable, literary, scientific, and other associations" was approved March 2, 1867.[19] This law repealed the act of 1862 which had been passed under the same title. However, it did not repeal the act of 1865 which provided for historic, scientific, and other literary societies, seemingly being intended to be supplementary to that law. Amendments were made to the 1867 act by the legislatures of 1873, 1941, and 1949.[20]

On March 4, 1867, "An Act for the incorporation of hospitals or asylums in certain cases" was approved.[21] This law, which provides for the method of incorporating, the powers of the corporation, regulations concerning the trustees, the funds of the corporation, and a tax exemption, has never been amended and stands on the books today in its original form.

The third state legislature of Nevada approved, March 5, 1869, an "Act to provide for the formation of corporations for the accumulation and investment of funds and savings."[22] While there is no express repeal of this act in ensuing corporation acts, the provisions it contains are covered by the general corporation law of 1925 and this act does not appear in Nevada Revised Statutes.

[17] BH.1020.
[18] BH. 834.
[19] BH. 1028.
[20] NRS. 86.100 ff.
[21] BH. 1037.
[22] BH. 948.

These first three legislatures apparently covered the field of corporation law satisfactorily for most of the needs of the new state. No new major legislation on corporations was enacted for thirty-two years after the third legislature, except for special acts for particular groups and some amendments and additions to the previous acts.[23]

On March 16, 1901, the Nevada legislature approved "An Act to provide for the incorporation, operation, and management of co-operative associations."[24] This act was amended in 1941.[25] It appears in the current Nevada Revised Statutes, as one of five acts which have been grouped together under the general title of nonprofit corporations.

The legislature of 1903 overhauled the old act of March 10, 1865, and approved, March 16, 1903, "An Act providing a general corporation law."[26] This act is the first in Nevada to be called a general corporation law. No specific former corporation law is repealed by this act. However, the act does contain a general repealer that "all acts and parts of acts, general and special, inconsistent or in conflict with this act are hereby repealed." The act of March 10, 1865, while not explicitly repealed, is certainly superseded by the 1903 act.[27] Similarly, inasmuch as the 1903 general corporation act contains several sections on the corporation of railroads, it can be said to supersede the former railroad corporation act of 1865. Finally all previous acts, approved for any purpose and not repealed elsewhere, must give way to the 1903 act on any point of conflict with the 1903 law.

The next corporation law was approved by the 1915 legislature on March 2. It was entitled "An Act to provide for the creation of corporations sole, and defining the powers thereof, and other matters relating to such corporations."[28] It is under this act that the Roman Catholic diocese of Reno is incorporated today. Accordingly, this act will receive more extensive treatment later in this work.[29] Amendments were made to the act in 1917, 1941, and 1949.[30]

[23] Some of these special acts are treated together at the end of this article. Cf. *infra*, pp. 29-30.

[24] RL. 1249.

[25] NRS. 18.200 ff.

[26] RL. 1105.

[27] Cf. *Revised Laws of Nevada (1912)* p. 105.

[28] NRS. 84.010 ff.

[29] Cf. *infra*, pp. 97-103.

[30] NRS. 84.010 ff.

"An Act to provide for the organization, management, and conduct of nonprofit cooperative corporations, providing for membership therein, and matters properly connected therewith" was approved by the state legislature March 23, 1921.[31] This act underwent amendments in 1931, 1939, 1941, and 1949.[32] It is one of the five acts currently grouped in Nevada Revised Statutes under the general title of nonprofit corporations.

The most recent general corporation law of Nevada was approved March 21, 1925.[33] This law, frequently amended (1929, 1931, 1935, 1937, 1939, 1941, 1945, 1949, 1955, 1957), contains the current general corporation provisions for Nevada. The legislature in 1935 attached a repealer to this act, whereby the general corporation law of 1903 was repealed. In repealing that law, the 1925 act also supersedes the still earlier laws which had also been superseded by the 1903 law. The 1925 law is entitled "An Act providing a general corporation law," and is found, as amended, in chapter 78 of the Nevada Revised Statutes.

In most recent years three corporation laws have been passed by Nevada legislatures. On March 22, 1945, the legislature approved "An Act to authorize the formation of nonprofit corporations for the purpose of engaging in charitable and eleemosynary activities, and prescribing the powers, operation, and management of such corporations, and other matters properly connected therewith."[34] On March 15, 1949, the legislature approved "An Act to authorize nonprofit corporations for the advancement of state and local interests."[35] On March 20, 1955, the legislature approved "An Act providing for nonstock, nonprofit cooperative corporations."[36] All three of these laws are currently carried in chapter 81 of Nevada Revised Statutes, together with the acts of 1901, and 1921, under the general heading of nonprofit corporations.

Nevada legislatures have also passed thirteen acts providing for the incorporation of specific churches, fraternal orders and other organizations. The first such act was approved at the first territorial

[31] NCL. 1575.
[32] NRS. 81.010 ff.
[33] NCL. 1600.
[34] NRS. 81.290.
[35] NRS. 81.350.
[36] NRS. 81.410.
[37] NRS. 82.300-82.390.

legislature in 1862. It provided special rules for the incorporation of Protestant Episcopal Churches.[37] Amendments and additions were made to this law in 1869, 1915 and 1919.[38] The first state legislature approved an act for the incorporation of the Free and Accepted Masons and the Independent Order of Odd Fellows.[39] In 1867 and 1947 amendments were made to the act.[40] The provisions of this act for the formation of the Masons and Odd Fellows as a corporation served as a model for the incorporation of several other organizations. Acts were approved by state legislatures for the incorporation of the Independent Order of Good Templars (1869),[41] The Irish American Benevolent Society (1877),[42] The Knights of Pythias (1883),[43] and the Benevolent Bachelor Brothers (1893),[44] and in each of these acts it was enacted that the rules for the formation and the powers of the corporation were to be taken from the act of 1865 providing for the incorporation of the Masons and Odd Fellows.

Acts for the incorporation of specific organizations were also approved for the following: The Ancient Order of Hibernians (1873),[45] The Women's Christian Temperance Union (1903),[46] Sigma Alpha Epsilon (1923),[47] the American Legion (1928),[48] the Boy Scouts of America (1929), [49] the Order of Nevadans (1931),[50] and the Veterans of Foreign Wars (1949).[51] Specific regulations for the formation, powers, trustees, and dissolution of these corporations was passed in these acts, none of which has since been amended.

ARTICLE 2. FORMATION OF CORPORATIONS

The most recent compilation of Nevada law, Nevada Revised Statutes, carries twelve different corporation acts. One of them is

[38] *Ibid.*
[39] NRS. 82.010-82.080.
[40] *Ibid.*
[41] NRS. 82.180.
[42] NRS. 82.100.
[43] NRS. 82.090.
[44] NRS. 82.170.
[45] NRS. 82.110.
[46] NRS. 82.400.
[47] NRS. 82.190.
[48] NRS. 82.520.
[49] NRS. 82.460.
[50] NRS. 82.240.
[51] NRS. 82.580.

actually the grouping of the special corporation acts for specific churches, fraternal orders, and other organizations. Since none of these specific acts treats of Catholic churches or organizations, they have no direct bearing on the purposes of this work and accordingly will be omitted from further consideration in this chapter. The other eleven acts are not so specific in nature, and, while some of them would scarcely be suitable for any needs of the Church or its institutions, for the sake of a more complete picture of Nevada corporation legislation, a brief review of the regulations of each of these eleven acts on formation will be included here, and a treatment of their powers and methods of dissolution will appear in the two succeeding articles. None of the acts expressly excludes churches from incorporating under them, although the very nature of the act would in some cases preclude such action.

Section I. General Corporation Law (1925)

Any number of persons, not less than three, may establish a corporation under the Nevada general corporation law. The purpose for which they incorporate may be to transact any lawful business or to promote or conduct any legitimate object or purpose. Formation of the corporation is achieved by executing, acknowledging, and filing in the office of the secretary of state articles of incorporation, and then filing, in the office of the clerk of the county in which the corporation's principal place of business will be located, a copy of the same articles of incorporation, certified under the hand and seal of the secretary of state.[52]

The articles of incorporation should contain the following information: the name of the corporation;[53] its address; the nature of its business, or its objects and purposes; the amount of the total authorized capital stock, the number and par value of shares, and a description of the classes of stock and the series in which they may be issued; the number, names, and addresses of the members of the first governing board and whether they are to be called directors or trustees; provisions for assessments upon the paid-up stock to pay debts of the corporation, if so desired; the name and address of each

[52] NRS. 78.030; as amended, Stats. 1931, 416.

[53] The name of the corporation must be such as to distinguish it from any other corporation in the state and shall end with the word "Incorporated," "Inc.," or "Ltd.," or shall contain the word "Association," "Company," "Co.," "Corporation, " "Corp.," "Club," "Society," "Syndicate," "Synd.," or "Union," used as a substantive noun or as part of the name of the corporation. NRS. 78.035; as amended, Stats. 1931, 416.

incorporator signing the articles; whether or not the corporation is to have perpetual existence, and, if not, the time when it is to cease; any other special provisions which the incorporators may wish to include concerning the operation of the corpration, the rights and duties of the corporation, its directors, or stockholders.[54]

The persons associating, their successors and assigns, shall be and constitute a body corporate from the date of the certificate, issued by the secretary of state, stating that the articles of incorporation have been filed in his office and contain all the required information.[55]

Section II. Cooperative Associations (1901)

Any five or more persons may legally form a cooperative association in Nevada for the purpose of transacting any lawful business. The association may not have or issue any capital stock; it must issue membership cards to each member, all of whole rights and interests are to be equal. Persons above eighteen years of age are eligible for membership.

To form such an association articles of incorporation must be prepared, containing the following information about the association: its name and purpose; the place where its principal business will be transacted; the term of its existence, which may not exceed fifty years; the number of trustees and the names and residences of the first trustees named; the amount of the fee for admission to membership and a statement that each member signing the articles has so paid; a statement that the interests and rights of all members will be equal.

These articles must be subscribed by the original associates or members, and acknowledged by each before an officer authorized to take acknowledgements of deeds in Nevada. The articles are then to be filed in the office of the secretary of state, who will furnish a copy thereof, which in turn must be filed in the office of the clerk of the county where the principal business of the association will be transacted. Upon the fulfillment of these filings of properly prepared articles of incorporation, the cooperative association enjoys the status of a corporation.[56]

[54] NRS. 78.035; as amended, Stats. 1931, 416; 1949, 158; 1955, 402; 1957, 75.
[55] NRS. 78.045.
[56] NRS. 81.180-81.200.

Section III. Nonprofit Cooperative Corporations (1921)

Nonprofit cooperative corporations may or may not have capital stock. They may be formed by three or more persons, the majority of whom must be Nevada residents. Formation of these corporations takes place, when properly executed articles of incorporation have been filed in the office of the secretary of state and a certificate to that effect has been filed in the office of the clerk of the county where the corporation's principal business will be transacted.

The articles of incorporation must contain: the name of the corporation; its purpose, the place where its principal business will be transacted; the term for which it is to exist, not to exceed fifty years; information concerning its capital stock and shares, if it has any; the names and addresses of its first directors; information concerning the voting power, property rights, and interest of each member; any other legal provisions concerning the government, financing, indebtedness, membership, etc., which the incorporators may wish to include.[57]

Section IV. Nonstock, Nonprofit Cooperative Corporations (1955)

Nonstock, nonprofit cooperative corporations may be formed by three or more persons, a majority of whom must be residents of Nevada. Such a corporation may hold no stock nor conduct business for profit. Its incorporators must prepare articles of incorporation containing: the name and purpose of the corporation; the place of its principal business; its term of existence, which may not exceed fifty years; the number of directors, not to be less than three; the names and residences of those named for the first year; whether the voting power and property rights and interest of each member shall be equal or unequal, and if the latter, how it is to be determined. These articles must be subscribed by three or more of the original members, acknowledged before an officer authorized to take acknowledgements of conveyances of real property, and filed in the office of the secretary of state, who shall issue a sealed certificate to that effect. A certified copy of the articles of incorporation must then be filed in the proper county clerk's office.[58]

[57] NRS. 81.015; as amended, Stats. 1941, 329; 1949, 635.

[58] NRS. 81.410-81.450.

Section V. Nonprofit Corporations for Advancement of State and Local Interests (1949)

This type of nonprofit corporation may be formed by five or more persons, who must be citizens of the United States and residents of Nevada, and who wish to associate for the advancement of civic, commercial, industrial, or agricultural interests of the state or any city, town or county in the state. To form the corporation, the associates must make, sign, acknowledge before an officer authorized to take acknowledgements, and file in the office of the secretary of state, written articles of incorporation containing: the name of the corporation; a statement that it is a nonprofit corporation solely for the advancement of civic, commercial, industrial, or agricultural interests of the state or a locality therein; the county in which the principal office will be located; the number of trustees, not less than five nor more than twenty-five; their term of office, which may not exceed six years, and the method by which they are to be chosen; the names and addresses of the trustees chosen for the first year. The secretary of state then issuses a certificate of the organization of the corporation, authenticated under his hand and seal, and a certified copy of it is filed in the proper county clerk's office.[59]

Section VI. Nonprofit Corporations for Charitable and Eleemosynary Activities (1945)

Charitable and eleemosynary corporations are also formed by executing articles of incorporation, filing them in the office of the secretary of state, and filing the latter's certificate to that effect in the office of the clerk of the county in which the principal office of the corporation is situated. These corporations may be formed by five or more persons, who must be United States citizens. Information in the articles of incorporation should include: the name of the corporation; a statement that it is a nonprofit corporation, organized solely for general charitable and eleemosynary purposes; the county in Nevada where its principal office will be located; the number of trustees, not less than three; their term of office and the method by which they are to be chosen; the names and addresses of the first trustees.[60]

[59] NRS. 81.350-81.360.

[60] NRS. 81.290-81.295; as amended, Stats. 1951, 320.

Section VII. Historic, Scientific, and Other Literary Societies (1865)

Corporations may be created for the organization and maintenance of gymnastic, athletic, historic, scientific and literary societies, designed to promote the diffusion of useful knowledge. Any five or more persons may make, sign, and acknowledge a certificate, which is to be filed in the office of the secretary of state. A copy of it is also to be filed in the proper county recorder's office. This certificate must contain: the corporate name of the society or association; its objects; the time of its existence, which may not exceed fifty years; the number and names of its directors, not more than five nor less than three; the name of the city or town in which the principal business of the corporation will be transacted.[61]

Section VIII. Cemetery Associations (1865)

The procedure required to form cemetery associations in Nevada is as follows. Any number of persons residing in this state, not less than five, are to meet, appoint a chairman and secretary by majority vote, determine a corporate name, the number of trustees, not less than six nor more than twelve, and immediately elect them by ballot. The trustees are to be divided by lot into three classes: those to hold office for one year, those to hold office for two years, and those to hold office for three years. Then it must be determined on what day in each year the election of trustees will be held. Within three days after this meeting, the chairman and secretary must make and sign a written certificate, and acknowledge it before an officer qualified to take proof and acknowledgement of conveyances in the county where the meeting was held. This certificate must contain the names of the associates determined upon by the majority of persons who met, the number of trustees, their names and classifications, and the date determined for the annual elections. The certificate must then be filed and recorded in the office of the clerk of the county in which the cemetery grounds are situated.[62]

Section IX. Hospitals and Charitable Asylums (1867)

The person or persons forming this type of corporation must execute, sign and acknowledge before an officer authorized in this state to take acknowledgements of deeds, duplicate articles of incor-

[61] NRS. 86.010-86.020.

[62] NRS. 83.010-83.020.

poration. One of them must be filed in the office of the secretary of state and the other one in the office of the clerk of the county in which the office of the corporation is situated. This type of corporation may be formed "where lands or any other property, amounting in value to one thousand dollars or upwards, have been or shall hereafter be given, granted, devised or bequeathed to one or more trustees, or persons acting in the capacity of trustees, for the purpose of founding or endowing a hospital, or other charitable asylum within this state, for the care and relief of orphan children, or of sick or indigent persons, and it shall, for the more effective and perfect administration of such trust, be deemed expedient by such trustee (s) to organize themselves as a corporation."[63]

The articles of incorporation must contain: the name of the corporation, the city, town or county in which the hospital or asylum is to be located, and the period for which it is incorporated; the object of the corporation; the names of the trustees; the number of persons constituting the permanent board of trustees, how the first board was elected or appointed, the time for which they were named and the method by which their successors are to be chosen; any other officers of the corporation; the date chosen to hold the annual meeting.[64]

Section X. Religious, Charitable, Literary, and Scientific Associations (1867)

Churches, congregations, religious, moral, beneficial, charitable, literary, or scientific associations or societies may incorporate in the following manner. The church, congregation, association, or society must first elect or appoint trustees or directors, not less than three nor more than fifteen, according to its own particular discipline. The trustees or directors are elected for the purpose of taking charge of the estate and property of the organization and to transact all affairs relative to the temporalities thereof.[65]

A certificate of this election or appointment is then executed by the person or persons making the appointment, or the judges holding the election, or the secretary of the association or society. This certificate must contain the names of the trustees or directors and the

[63] NRS. 85.010.
[64] NRS. 85.015.
[65] NRS. 86.010.

name by which the association is to be called. The certificate must then be acknowledged before an officer authorized to take acknowledgements of deeds. Formation of the corporation takes place, when this certificate, together with a certificate of its acknowledgement, is recorded by the clerk of the county in which the organization is situated.[66]

Section XI. Corporations Sole (1915)

A corporation sole is formed in the following manner.[67] Written articles of incorporation, in duplicate, are to be executed, signed, and acknowledged before an officer authorized to take acknowledgements. One of these articles of incorporation must be filed in the office of the secretary of state, and the other one is to be kept in the possession of the person who made and signed it. Such articles of incorporation may be made by "any person being the archbishop, bishop, president, trustee in trust, president at stake, president of congregation, overseer, presiding elder, district superintendent, or other presiding officer or clergyman, of any church or religious society or denomination, who may have been duly chosen, elected, or appointed, in conformity with the constitution, canons, rites, regulations, or discipline of a church or religious society, and in whom shall be vested the legal title to property held for the purposes, use, or benefit, of such church or religious society."[68]

The articles of incorporation must contain: the name of the corporation, which must include the name or offiice of the person making the articles and end with "a corporation sole";[69] its object; the estimated value of its property at the time of making the articles of incorporation; the title of the person making the articles and the manner in which any vacancy in his office is to be filled.[70]

ARTICLE 3. POWERS OF CORPORATIONS

Section I. General Corporation Law (1925)

Fundamental powers granted by Nevada's general corporation law include those which such a corporation has by virtue of its very

[66] NRS. 86.015-86.020.

[67] The act states that "Corporations may be formed for acquiring, holding, or disposing of church or religious society property, for the benefit of religion, for works of charity, and for public worship, in the manner herein after provided in this chapter." NRS. 84.010.

[68] NRS. 84.015; as amended, Stats. 1949, 283.

[69] Cf. Attorney General Opinion #843, December 30, 1949.

[70] NRS. 84.020; as amended, Stats. 1917, 22.

existence, such as: to have succession by its corporate name, perpetually, or for the period limited in its articles of incorporation, or until dissolved by law; to sue and be sued in any court of law or equity; to make contracts; to adopt, use, and alter at pleasure a common seal; to hold, purchase, convey, mortgage, or lease real and personal estate; to take real and personal estate, except in the case of religious corporations, by devise or bequest in this state or any other state, territory or country; to appoint and compensate officers and agents of the corporation as needed; to make by-laws for the management, regulation, and government of the corporation's affairs and property, the transfer of its stock, transaction of its business, calling and holding stockholders' meetings, provided that these by-laws are not inconsistent with the constitution or laws of the United States or Nevada; to dissolve itself.[71]

Other powers granted by this law, but subject to any limitations which may be contained in a particular corporation's articles of incorporation or in amendments to those articles, include the power: to borrow money and contract debts; to issue bonds, promissory notes, etc.; to dispose of the shares of its own capital stock or that of others, while owner of such stock by guarantee, purchase, hold, sale, assign, transfer, mortgage, or pledge; to conduct business, have one or more offices, hold, purchase, mortgage, and convey real and personal property in Nevada or anywhere else; and to do whatever is necessary and proper in order to accomplish the objects of the corporation or to protect and benefit it.[72]

Section II. Cooperative Associations (1901)

Among the powers of cooperative associations are: to sue and be sued in the associate name; to receive by gift, devise, or purchase, to hold and convey, real and personal property, as the purposes of the association require; to appoint agents and officers as required to admit associates or members; to sell or forfeit their interest in the association for default of installments, dues, work or labor required, as provided in the by-laws; to enter into any and all lawful contracts of obligations essential to the transaction of its affairs, for the purpose for which the association was formed; to borrow money; to issue all such

[71] NRS. 78.060.

[72] NRS. 78.070. More specific powers for particular kinds of corporations, such as, railroads, municipalities, various types of stock companies, etc., are also contained in the general corporation law, but these are not pertinent to this study.

notes, bills, or evidence of indebtedness or mortgage, as its by-laws may provide; to trade, barter, sell, and exchange; to do all things proper to be done in order to carry into effect the objects of the association.[73]

Section III. Nonprofit Cooperative Corporations (1921)

The nonprofit cooperative corporation act of 1921 divides the powers of such corporations into three groups. The first group of powers concerns agents, officers and membership, and rules that these corporations may: appoint persons or corporations as agents and officers according as their business requires it; admit and expel persons and corporations to membership according to the provisions of their by-laws; forfeit membership to any member for violation of the by-laws. The second group of powers treats property and contracts, and declares that these corporations have the power "to purchase, lease or otherwise acquire, hold, own, and enjoy; to sell, lease, mortgage, and otherwise encumber and dispose of any and all and every kind of real and personal property; also to carry on any and all operations necessary or convenient in connection with the transactions of any of its business." Detailed descriptions of these corporations' contracting powers are also contained in this group. The third group of powers considers the special situation in which two such associations may wish to consolidate in order to carry on their business, and lists the conditions under which such consolidation may be effected and the rights and duties stemming from such a consolidation.[74]

Section IV. Nonstock, Nonprofit Cooperative Corporations (1955)

Powers granted nonstock, nonprofit cooperative corporations are: to appoint such agents and officers, either persons or corporations, as the business of the corporation requires; to admit both persons and corporations to membership; to expel members, in accordance with the by-laws; to forfeit the membership of any member for the violation of any agreement between him and the corporation or for his violation of the by-laws; to purchase, lease, or otherwise acquire, hold, own, and enjoy; to sell, lease, mortgage and otherwise encumber and dispose of any and all and every kind of real and personal property; to carry on all operations necessary and convenient

[73] NRS. 81.220.

[74] NRS. 81.050; as amended, Stats. 1941, 331.

for the transaction of its business. Also, the powers granted by the provisions of other laws of Nevada relating to private corporations are granted to these corporations, provided they are not inconsistent with any provisions specifically made for these corporations.[75]

Section V. Nonprofit Corporations for the Advancement of State and Local Interests (1949)

These corporations have the power: to receive, acquire, hold, manage, administer, and expend property and funds for the general and specific purposes of the corporation; to take property by will, gift, or otherwise for the general and specific purposes of the corporations; to hold, in its own name and right, real and personal property, with no limitation to extent, and with the same powers of management, control, etc., as a private person, subject, however, to the terms of any particular trusts; to borrow money, upon or without security, giving promissory notes or other evidences of indebtedness and mortgages, pledges, and other instruments of hypothecation; to appoint and pay officers and agents, so long as no compensation is given to any members of the board of trustees; to adopt by-laws; and to do any and all things which a natural person might do necessary and desirable for the general purposes of the corporations.[76]

Section VI. Nonprofit Corporations for Charitable and Eleemosynary Activities (1945)

Charitable and eleemosynary corporations are given the following powers, which they may exercise without obtaining any court order: to receive, acquire, hold, manage, administer, and expend property and funds by will, gift, or otherwise, so long as it is held for a charitable and eleemosynary purpose; to hold, in its own name and right, real and personal property of every nature, similar to the absolute ownership of a private person, subject, however, to the terms of particular trusts and to the general trust that all its property shall be held for charitable and eleemosynary purposes; to borrow money, either upon or without security, giving such promissory notes or other evidences of indebtedness and such pledges, mortgages or other instrutments of hypothecation as it may be advised; to appoint and pay officers and agents, so long as no member of the board of trus-

[75] NRS. 81.500.
[76] NRS. 81.370.

tees receives any compensation; to adopt by-laws; to do any and all things which a natural person might do necessary and desirable for the general purpose of the corporation; to receive and use funds obtained from private donations, devises and bequests, and from all lawful sources to be applied for charitable and eleemosynary purposes.[77]

Section VII. Historic, Scientific, and Other Literary Societies (1865)

Powers of these corporations include the following: to sue and be sued, and prosecute and defend in any court; to devise, adopt, and use a seal, and change the same at pleasure; to purchase, accept by grant, gift or devise, hold, sell, and convey such real and personal property, or estate, as the purpose of the society or association may require; to appoint or elect and remove such officers, agents, and servants as the business of the society requires; to define their powers, prescribe their duties, and fix their compensation; to make by-laws not inconsistent with the constitution and laws of this state, for the transaction of the business of the association, the management of its property, the regulations of its affairs, the admission and expulsion of its members, and generally for the transaction of all such business as may be within the scope of its organization and original design.[78]

The power of these corporations to contract indebtedness is limited by this law to the sum of one thousand dollars. They may not, by any implication or construction, be deemed to possess the power of issuing bills, notes, or other evidence of debt for circulation as money.[79]

Section VIII. Cemetery Associations (1865)

Legally incorporated cemetery associations have the power: to sue and be sued in any court; to make,use, and alter at pleasure a common seal; to purchase, hold, sell, and convey such real and personal estate as is required by the association's purposes; to appoint officers, agents, and servants, as the business of the corporation requires, and to define their powers, remove them at will, except trustees, who can be removed only by a two-thirds vote of all the trustees or by a majority vote of the trustees upon a written request signed by half of the

[77] NRS. 81.310.

[78] NRS. 86.040.

[79] NRS. 86.080.

lot owners; to make by-laws which are not inconsistent with the laws of Nevada; to take by purchase or devise, and hold, within the county in which the certificate of their incorporation is recorded, no more than three hundred and twenty acres of land, to be held and occupied exclusively for a cemetery, for the burial of the dead; to hold personal property, not exceeding five thousand dollars, besides what may arise from the sale of lots and plots.[80]

Section IX. Hospitals and Charitable Asylums (1867)

The powers of incorporated hospitals and charitable asylums include these: to sue and be sued; to take, hold, and convey real and personal estate by gift, grant devise, or bequest, but only for the purposes for which it was incorporated, and only such lands as are necessary for the direct and reasonable use or convenience of the hospital or asylum may be held for a period longer than ten years; to adopt and change a comon seal; and to exercise all the powers and be subject to all the responsibilities conferred and imposed by law.[81]

Section X. Religious, Charitable, Literary and Scientific Associations (1867)

The trustees or directors of associations incorporated under this act have the following powers: to have and alter at pleasure a common seal; to possess and protect all the temporalities of the corporation; to sue and be sued; to receive and hold all debts, demands, rights, and privileges; to receive and hold all churches, burying places, halls, school houses, hospitals, or other buildings, necessary to carry out the objects of the association; to perform all the duties imposed upon them by the regulations, rules, or discipline of the association.[82]

The powers of these corporations are limited by the act in their rights to property holdings. They may not sell or mortgage their real estate without first obtaining a court order, and approval of the court is needed before they can direct the application of moneys received from such a sale to the interests of the corporations.[83]

80 NRS. 83.030-83.040.
81 NRS. 85.010, 85.040.
82 NRS. 86.120.
83 NRS. 86.130; as amended, Stats. 1949, 55.

Another limitation on these corporations concerns the amount of real estate which they may hold. In a town or city such a corporation's real estate may not exceed one block, and in the country it is limited to ten acres. However, the orders of Free and Accepted Masons, and the Independent Order of Odd Fellows, and their subordinate lodges, are excepted for this limitation.[84]

Section XI. Corporations Sole (1915)

A corporation sole in Nevada has the following powers: to acquire and possess, by donation, gift, bequest, devise, or purchase, and to hold and maintain real, personal, and mixed property; to grant, sell, convey, rent, or otherwise dispose of its property; to borrow money and give promissory notes or some other written obligation therefore, and to secure payment thereof by mortgage or other lien, upon real or personal property; to buy, sell, lease, mortgage, and in every way deal in personal property in the same manner that a natural person may, and without the order of any court; to receive bequests and devises for its own use or upon trusts, just as natural persons may; to appoint attorneys in fact; to contract and be contracted with; to sue and be sued, plead and be pleaded in all courts of justice; to have and use a common seal, by which all the acts and deeds of such corporation may be authenticated.[85]

Article 4. Dissolution Of Corporations

Section I. General Corporation Law (1925)

Nevada's general corporation law treats of three principal methods by which corporations may be dissolved. They are by expiration of the charter, by court order, and by voluntary dissolution. If the articles of incorporation name a time at which the corporation is to cease to exist, the corporation is automatically dissolved upon the arrival of the determined date. Upon application to the district court by any holder or holders of one-tenth of the issued and outstanding capital stock, the district court may order the corporation dissolved and appoint a receiver to wind up its affairs. This application may be made only when one of the following situations is verified: the corporation has willfully violated its charter; its trustee or directors have been guilty of fraud or collusion or gross mismanagement in

[84] NRS. 86.160. Cf. *infra*, pp. 107-108.

[85] NRS. 84.050.

the conduct of its affairs, or misfeasance, malfeasance, or nonfeasance, or they have been unable to conduct the business or conserve the corporation's assets on account of an act, neglect, or refusal to function on the part of any of the directors or trustees; the assets of the corporation are in danger of waste, sacrifice, or loss through attachment, foreclosure, litigation, or otherwise; the corporation has abandoned its business, or has not proceeded diligently to wind up its affairs, or to distribute its assets in a reasonable time; the corporation has become insolvent, or, although not insolvent, is for any cause not able to pay its debts or other obligations as they mature, or is not about to resume its business with safety to the public.[86]

A corporation may voluntarily dissolve itself in the following manner. Its board of trustees adopts a resolution to dissolve and calls a meeting of the stockholders with voting power to decide the issue. If the holders of stock entitled to exercise two-thirds of all the voting power of the corporation resolve that the corporation should be dissolved, a copy of such resolution is to be filed in the office of the secretary of state. Filed with the resolution should be the names and addresses of the directors, certified by the president, or a vice-president, and the secretary, or an assistant secretary, and the treasurer, or an assistant treasurer. The secretary of state then issues a certificate that the corporation has been dissolved. A corporation may also be dissolved voluntarily, whenever stockholders having nine-tenths of the voting power consent in writing to a dissolution. In this case, no meeting of the stockholders is required, but the secretary of state may issue the certificate of dissolution upon receiving the written consent.[87]

Corporations which have been dissolved by any of these methods remain corporate bodies for three years for the purpose of prosecuting and defending suits by or against them, and to enable them to settle their business, dispose of property, divide capital stock, but not for the purpose of continuing the business for which the corporation was established.[88]

The act also provides for the dissolution of a corporation before it has begun the operation of the business for which it was incorporated. The incorporators must file in the office of the secretary of

[86] NRS. 78.650.
[87] NRS. 78.580.
[88] NRS. 78.590.

state a certificate that no part of the capital has been paid and that the business has not been started. The certificate must be verified by the oath or affirmation of a majority of the incorporators named in the articles of incorporation. The corporation is dissolved with the filing of this certificate.[89]

Section II. Cooperative Associations (1901)

Besides being dissolved by the expiration of its charter, a co-operative association, incorporated under this act, may be dissolved voluntarily in the following manner. Two-thirds of the members must request the dissolution. This request must be addressed to the directors and must specify the reasons on account of which the dissolution is deemed desirable. The request must name three persons, who are members, to act in liquidation and in winding up the affairs of the association. Thereupon, a majority of these three persons shall have full power to do all things necessary for liquidation. Upon filing the request with the directors and filing a copy of it in the office of the clerk of the county in which the association's principal business is transacted, all powers of the directors shall cease. The persons named will then proceed to wind up the affairs of the association, pay all debts, divide the residue among the members, "share and share alike," within the time named in the written request. If needed, the time may be lengthened by two-thirds of the members by filing a written request in the county clerk's office.[90]

Section III. Nonprofit Cooperative Corporations (1921)

Nonprofit cooperative corporations are not established as perpetual corporations. Their articles of incorporation must specify the term for which they are to exist, a period which is not to exceed fifty years. Accordingly, such a corporation is dissolved by the expiration of its charter at the time specified in its articles of incorporation.

These corporations may also be dissolved voluntarily by the written consent of members representing two-thirds of the total votes. The exact manner of this voluntary dissolution is to be the same as that provided for in the act of 1901 for cooperative associations, except that any property remaining after liquidation is to be

[89] NRS. 78.585.

[90] NRS. 81.280.

divided among the members according to their respective property interests therein.[91]

Section IV. Nonstock, Nonprofit Cooperative Corporations (1955)

Nonstock, nonprofit cooperative corporations may not exist for a term exceeding fifty years and are dissolved by the expiration of their charters at the time specified in their articles of incorporation. They may also be dissolved voluntarily by the written consent of members representing two-thirds of the total vote. The manner in which this dissolution is effected is the same as that enacted for co-operative associations (1901) and described in NRS. 81.280.[92]

Section V. Historic, Scientific, and Other Literary Societies (1865)

This act contains no specific statute concerning the method of dissolution for these corporations. However, since the act rules that these corporations may not exist more than fifty years, it is clear that they are dissolved by the expiration of their charter on the date named in their articles of incorporation or fifty years after incorporation, if no date of expiration is named in the articles. The law itself provides no method for voluntary dissolution, but should the incorporators outline such a procedure in the articles of incorporation, it seems that such voluntary dissolution would be legal. The act does point out that, if it should happen that an election of directors should not be made on the day designated by the society's by-laws, the corporation shall not for that reason be dissolved.[93]

Section VI. Nonprofit Corporations for Advancement of State and Local Interests (1949), Nonprofit Corporations for Charitable and Eleemosynary Activities (1945), Cemetery Associations (1867), Hospitals and Charitable Asylums (1867), Religious, Charitable, Literary, and Scientific Associations (1867), Corporations Sole (1915)

In the acts providing for the establishment of all the corporations mentioned in the title to this section, no reference is made to any method of dissolution. These corporations are more generally

[91] NRS. 78.050. Cf. *supra*, p. 45.
[92] NRS. 81.520. Cf. *supra*, p. 45.
[93] NRS. 86.060.

of a perpetual nature. However, if any of these corporations should in its articles of incorporation name a period of time during which it is to exist, it would be dissolved by the expiration of its charter at the end of the specified period. Similarly, the articles of incorporation or the by-laws could declare particular regulations for the voluntary dissolution of any of these corporations, if the incorporators or members so desired. There is nothing in the law to prevent such action on their part. However, the law itself provides no general enactment for their dissolution by any means.

The general perpetuity of corporations sole is recognized by the Nevada law in an enactment specifying that in the event of the death or removal from office of that person who is the corporation sole, his successor in office, as such corporation sole, shall be vested with the same powers and title to property and subject to the same liabilities as his predecessor. A certified copy of his commission, certificate, or letter of election or appointment is to be filed in the office of the county recorder of each county in which any of the property of the corporation sole is situated. Thus, instead of passing any rules for their dissolution, the law specifically provides for the perpetuity of corporations sole.[94]

[94] NRS. 84.080.

CHAPTER III

ACQUISITION OF CHURCH PROPERTY

The Nevada Constitution has taken cognizance of the freedom of religion in these words:

> The free exercise and enjoyment of religious profession and worship without discrimination or preference shall forever be allowed in this State, and no person shall be rendered incompetent to be a witness on account of his opinions on matters of his religious belief, but the liberty of conscience hereby secured, shall not be so construed, as to excuse acts of licentiousness or justify practices inconsistent with the peace, or safety of this State.[1]

Man's inalienable rights are guaranteed in Nevada's Constitution thus: "All men are, by nature, free and equal, and have certain inalienable rights, among which are those of enjoying and defending life and liberty; acquiring, possessing and protecting property, and pursuing and obtaining safety and happiness."[2]

The Church, as a juridic moral person, claims the same rights and freedoms as the Nevada Constitution legally secures for natural men. As a perfect society, the Church claims these rights as her own, independent of any civil authority. The concern of this work is the Church's acquisition, tenure and administration of property. A survey of both Church and civil law on the acquisition of Church property with a view to the similarities and differences between the two, is the burden of this chapter.

ARTICLE I. ACQUISITION IN THE CODE OF CANON LAW

Section I. Church Property

The meaning of the term *Church property* is essential to a clear understanding of the legislation concerning it in the Code. The word *Church* in these canons refers not only to the Universal Church and the Apostolic See, but also to every moral person in the Church, unless the opposite is evident from the context or from the nature of the matter under discussion.[3]

1 Art. I, Sec. 4.

2 Art. I, Sec. 1.

3 Canon 1498.

Thus every ecclesiastical moral person, such as a diocese, parish, hospital, school, religious institute, is included when the Code uses the word *Church* in the canons treating acquisition, tenure, and administration of property. However, when the context or subject matter makes it apparent, *Church* may refer exclusively to the Universal Church and Apostolic See. Groups, such as the St. Vincent de Paul Society, the Knights of Columbus, etc., are not included in the term *Church,* and their property is not to be classified as ecclesiastical goods in the sense of these canons.

Church property or ecclesiastical goods[4] is defined by the Code as all temporal goods, incorporeal and corporeal, movable and immovable, which belong to the Universal Church and Apostolic See or to some other moral person in the Church.[5] Incorporeal property, that which is imperceivable by the senses, includes legal rights to corporeal property, such as, proprietary rights in the land of another, copyrights, stocks, rents, easements. Corporeal property is that which can be perceived by the senses, such as a rectory, hospital, or school. If corporeal property cannot be moved from place to place, it is immovable, as an acre of land or a building. Legally immovable property includes the windows, doors, and fixtures of a building and even the key to it.[6] Movable property is that which can be transferred from place to place. It is fungible, when it is designed generally, in kind, e. g., another object of the same kind. It is non-fungible, when it is designated specifically, for itself, e. g., the very same object.

Church property may be further divided into sacred things and precious things. Church property is sacred, when, by consecration or blessing, it is destined for divine worship. It is precious, when it takes on some notable value because of its artistic quality, historic worth, or the material from which it was made.[7] Authors generally hold that any object worth less than one thousand gold francs, or about $167, is not precious.[8] However, it is difficult to evaluate in

[4] The two terms are used synonymously in this work.

[5] Canon 1497,§1.

[6] Bouscaren, p. 799; Abbo-Hannan, *The Sacred Canons: A Concise Presentation of the Current Disciplinary Norms of the Church* (2 vols., St. Louis: B. Hender Book Company, 1952), II, 708 (hereafter cited Abbo-Hannan).

[7] Canon 1497,§2.

[8] Abbo-Hannan, II, 708; cf. Vermeersch-Creusen, *Epitome Iuris Canonici* (3 vols., Vol. II, 7. ed., 1949. Mechliniae-Romae: H. Dessain), II, n. 819 (hereafter cited Vermeersch-Creusen); DeMeester, *Iuris Canonici et Iuris Canonico-civilis Compendium* (3 Vols. in 4, Brugis: Descles. 1921-1928. III. no. 1446 (hereafter cited DeMeester).

terms of money things whose value is artistic or historical. Whereas the monetary worth of such objects may not be great in the open market, they may have very great importance to a particular church or religious group. Accordingly, the opinion of experts would be necessary to determine their special value.[9]

Section II. The Church's Right to Acquire Property

The Church's right to acquire property is an inherent right stemming from the nature of the Church as a perfect society. The Church is a moral person by divine institution, not by any civil enactment. Accordingly, it holds, acquires, and administers its temporal goods, freely and independently of civil authority, as its own natural right. The Code states that the "Catholic Church and Apostolic See have a natural right to acquire, own, and administer temporal property for the attainment of her proper ends, and this right is held freely and independently of civil power."[10]

Subordinate moral persons in the Church, such as dioceses, parishes, etc., receive their moral personality from ecclesiastical authority, and as properly created moral persons in the Church also enjoy the right to acquire, hold, and administer temporal things.[11]

As a perfect society, also, the Church has the right to support itself by demanding from the faithful "whatever is necessary for divine worship, for the adequate maintenance of the clergy and other ministers, and for her other proper purposes."[12]

Throughout her long history, the Church has always exercised this natural right in so far as she has been able, although she has not always been in a position to assert it openly as her right. There is evidence of actual ownership and management of temporal property by Church authorities even in Apostolic times. Christ and His Apostles had temporal goods, which they used for their support and for the aid of the poor. Judus Iscariot was their treasurer.[13] In its very first stages the Church accepted offerings from the faithful and put them into a common fund, which was considered the property of the society rather than that of the individuals and used for the needs of

[9] Bouscaren, p. 800.

[10] Canon 1495,§1; Cappelo, *Summa Iuris Canonici*: (3 vols, Vol., II, 4 ed., *Romae: Apud Aedes Universitatis Gregorianae,* 1945), II, 546 (hereafter cited Cappelo).

[11] Canon 1495,§2.

[12] Canon 1496.

[13] Cf. Mark, 6:37; Luke, 9:13; John, 4:8, 12:16, 13:29.

the society and the assistance of the needy.[14] The early Christians did not continue to hold all their property in common, but they did turn a portion into a general fund for the care of the poor and the support of the clergy. The church also acquired real property in the first centuries. Evidence of the Church's ownership of cemeteries, houses, places of worship, as well as movable goods can be found in the early writers and historians.[15] Roman civil law did not recognize the Church as a legitimate society at the time, but the emperors themselves did realize that the organization held real and personal property. Gallienus (260-268) and Gallerius (305-311) restored real property, notably cemeteries and churches, to the Church. Seemingly, they considered the property as that of the Church, rather than of individuals, since they restored the property to the bishops.[16] However, as a forbidden society, the Church was unable to express or openly claim her right to temporal property until after the edict of Constantine in 313. Constantine acknowledged the Church's proprietary rights, restoring property to the churches as such and to the society of Christians, as well as to individual Christians. The emperor was not bestowing a new right on the Church, but recognizing a right which the Church had always possessed and tried to exercise as far as had been possible.[17]

During the fourth and fifth centuries civil law not only recognized the right of the Church to acquire property, but granted such holdings special privileges. The Church could acquire property by donation, will, or any other "lucrative title." The property of one entering a monastery became the property of the monastery. Clerics who died intestate were considered to have left their property to the church to which they had been attached. The property of a person who ravished a consecrated virgin was seized as a penalty and turned over to the church to which the virgin was attached.[18]

Not only did civil law acknowledge the right of the Church to acquire temporal goods, but the Church also, now that her days of

[14] Acts, 2:44; 4:34-37; 5:4; 6:1-6.

[15] Goodwine, *The Right of the Church to Acquire Temporal Goods,* The Catholic University of America Canon Law Studies, N. 131 (Washington, D. C.: The Catholic University of America Press, 1941), pp. 56-58. (hereafter cited Goodwine).

[16] *Loc. cit.*; Scheys, *De Iure Ecclesiae Acquirendi et Possidenei Bona Temporalia* (Louvain: 1892), p. 107.

[17] Goodwine, p. 59; Augustine, *Commentary on Canon Law,* Vol. VI, *Administrative Law* (2 ed., St. Louis: B. Herder Book Co., 1923) p. 552.

[18] Goodwine, pp. 60-61.

persecution were ended and she was able to speak out openly, expressed this right in her own legislation. The right of the Church to temporal goods destined for pious uses was claimed at the Council of Ancyra (314)[19] and the Council of Antioch (341).[20] The Council of Vaison (442)[21] and the II Council of Arles (443)[22] both expressed the Church's right to acquire property and declared that it was a sacrilege not to deliver to the Church property which had been left it by will. The Council of Agde (506) reminded bishops that they were to consider property given for pious uses as given to the Church and not to them personally and stated that the right of the Church to possess property was to be carefully safeguarded by those who managed it.[23] The Church goods are not subject to civil prescription was claimed at the I Council of Orleans (511).[24] Many councils in the fifth and sixth centuries enacted canons stressing the right of the Church to acquire and hold property independently of civil authority and in no way subject to lay control or interference.[25]

About 696 King Withtred of Kent expressed a strong recognition of the proprietary rights of the Church, when he declared that no laymen should appropriate to himself "a church or any of the things which to a Church belong," and continued, "and therefore strongly and faithfully we appoint and decree, and in the name of Almighty God, and of all the saints we forbid to all kings, our successors, and to all eldermen, and to all laymen, ever any lordship over churches and over any of their possessions which I or my predecessors in days of old have given for the glory of Christ, and Our Lady St. Mary and the Holy Apostles."[26]

The right of the Church to acquire property was also brought out in the legislation of the early general councils of the Church. The I Council of Constantinople (381) legislated that Church pro-

[19] Hardouin, *Acta Conciliorum et Epistolae Decretales* (12 vols., 1715: Parisilis), I, 327 (hereafter cited Hardouin).

[20] Hardouin, I, 603, 606.

[21] Hardouin, I, 1788.

[22] Hardouin, II, 777.

[23] Hardouin, II, 998.

[24] Hardouin, II, 1011.

[25] Cf. I Council of Orleans, (511)-Hardouin II, 1009,; Council of Clermont-Auvergne (535)-Hardouin, II, 1181; Council of Lerida (546)-c.l, C. X, q.l; III Council of Paris (557)-Mansi, *Sacrorum Conciliorum nova et amplissima collectio* (53 vols., 1901-1927: Parisilis), IX, 743 (hereafter cited Mansi).

[26] Goodwine, p. 64; Haddan and Stubbs, *Councils and Ecclesiastical Documents relating to Great Britain and Ireland* (3 vols., Oxford, 1869-1873), III, 244.

perty should be administered by bishops.[27] The Council of Chalcedon (451) spoke of the Church's exercise of its right to acquire property, laid down rules for its protection during the vacancy of benefices, and forbade its conversion to secular purposes.[28] The administration of Church property was treated at the II Council of Nicaea (787)[29] and the IV Council of Constantinople (869-870), the latter council making an explicit distinction between church property and the property of churchmen and stressing the independence of church property.[30]

The I Lateran Council (1123), seeking to end the long-lived, much-attacked abuse of lay investiture, stressed that the Church's rights in property were hers by nature and had not been conferred on her by any civil authority, that lay persons had no power to dispose of the goods of the Church, the administration of which belonged to the bishops, and that it was sacrilegious for laymen of any rank to take over the disposition, control, or ownership of Church property.[31] These points were emphasized again in the II Lateran Council (1139) and the III Lateran Council (1179), as efforts were continuing to remove all vestiges of the practice of lay investiture.[32]

The right of the Church to acquire temporal goods without interference from secular princes, the fact that this right of the Church comes from a source higher than civil law, the distinction between the personal property of bishops and pastors and the property of their benefices, the claim that the Church holds property by natural right, can accept gifts from the faithful and succeed to the property of clerics who die intestate, the insistence that the bishop is to be the administrator of church property in the diocese and that no lay power could exercise any administrative power over such property—all these points were considered in the collections of law of Burchard of Worms (1025), Anselm of Lucca (1086), Ivo of Chartres (1116), and in the *Decretum Gratiani* (c. 1140).[33]

Furthermore, the mortmain laws, which did not deny the Church's right to acquire property but placed a severe limitation on

[27] Hardouin, I, 808-811.
[28] Hardouin, II, 601, 604, 609, 612.
[29] Hardouin, IV, 494-495.
[30] Hardouin, V, 905, 907.
[31] Mansi, XXI, 282.
[32] Mansi, XXI, 532; XXII, 225.
[33] Cf. Goodwine, pp. 67-70.

that right, were also vigorously opposed by the popes. Alexander III, (1159-1181), Alexander IV (1254-1261), and Boniface VIII (1294-1303), in particular, sought to put an end to these mortmain statutes, which they declared unjust, hostile to the interests of the Church, and null and void unless especially allowed by the pope in a concordat with the government. After Boniface VIII, the popes generally sought in their concordats with various countries to revoke all the old mortmain laws existant in that nation.[34] Implied, of course, in these efforts to destroy mortmain laws is a claim of the Church's right to acquire, hold, and administer temporal property independently of the civil government.

The Church found further opportunity to express her claim to the right to acquire property in her defense against medieval heresies. The Waldenses, Albigenses, Fraticelli, Wycliffites, and Lombards, among their other errors, held that the acquisition and possession of temporal goods by the Church and by clergymen was contrary to the teachings of Sacred Scripture.[35] The political philosophers, John of Jandun (1328) and Marsilius of Padua (1342), taught that all temporal goods held by the Church belonged by right to the civil authorities, who could reclaim them at will and through whose authorization alone they were acquired by the Church.[36] In condemning these teachings, the Church upheld once again her native right to acquire property independently of any civil power.

The spoliation of Church property by secular powers occasioned strong insistence by the Church that her natural rights be observed by the various States. The Council of Trent (1545-1563) decreed excommunications for those who usurped ecclesiastical property, took the tithes which were due to the Church or tried to turn Church holdings to their own profit.[37] However, in the centuries following, numerous civil rulers restricted or denied altogether the Church's right in property. Secular rulers acted upon the doctrine, an outgrowth of Richerianism and Febronianism,[38] that the Church could acquire property only with the permission of the State, because the Church received its juridical personality from the civil law. Accordingly, the popes were forced to defend again and again the contrary doctrine

[34] *Op. cit.*, pp. 71-73.
[35] *Op. cit.*, pp. 13-18.
[36] *Op. cit.*, p. 40.
[37] *Op. cit.*, p. 79.
[38] Cf. Tarquini, *Iuris Eccleiastic Publici Institutiones* ARomae: 1875), II, 7.

that as a perfect society the Church enjoyed its rights in property by nature and not by any concession of civil authority. During the eighteenth and nineteenth centuries concordats were reached with the rulers of France, Spain, Portugal, Italy, Germany, Austria, and others, which guaranteed these natural rights of the Church, only to have the agreements soon broken by a succeeding ruler of the country. Much Church property was lost through the wholesale secularization of Church goods, practiced by some rulers. Some of these properties were later returned by new governments; others seemingly have passed from the hands of the Church for good.[39]

Most recent concordats with the various nations recognize the right of the Church to acquire temporal possessions. Goodwine notes that a new trend seems to be developing in some recent concordats, for example those with Austria (1934), Prussia (1929), Germany (1933), in which the civil government agrees that the property rights of the Church will be "guaranteed according to the civil law of the State," and sees a possible misunderstanding arising from such terminology. He writes:

> There is no explicit mention of the native right of the Church but the right to acquire is recognized within the limits allowed by the civil law. Can it be argued, from this silence about the native right, that the Church in these cases has renounced its native right and that in these countries the right of the Church to acquire is derived from the civil law? The wording of the concordats might seem to indicate that the right of the Church to acquire is actually derived from the State since only those possessions of the Church are guaranteed and protected which have been or will be in accordance with the laws of the country.
>
> The traditional stand of the Church, as evidenced by history, is opposed to such a conclusion, however. The Church has consistently upheld its right to acquire, and has ever defended its independence from civil power. The purpose of concordats, moreover, is to assure that independence. Were the Church to submit to the pretensions of the State as to the right to acquire property its independence would be doomed.

[39] Cf. Goodwine, pp. 76-93, for details of these concordats.

If such a conclusion were allowed the concordats would openly conflict with the canon law of the Church. Since the promulgation of the Code it has been the desire of the Holy See that all new particular legislation should accord with the canons as much as possible. In view of this it is inconceivable that the Holy See would renounce or even comppromise a right that is of so fundamental importance.

What then does the restrictive phrasing of these recent concordats signify? It means that in the concordats the Holy See, while maintaining the right of the Church to acquire, agrees to comply with the formalities of the civil law in order to provide greater security for her possessions. If ecclesiastical goods have been acquired according to the civil law the Church is enabled to defend them even in civil courts.

This explanation accords with the explanation of the concordat with Ecuador given by Pius X to the bishops of that country in 1905. The concordat with Ecuador had recognized the right of the Church to acquire property by every just title consonant with the laws of the Republic. When the property of the Church was appropriated in violation of the provisions of the concordat, the pope reminded the people of Ecuador that the Church did not thereby lose its property; that the Church could still legitimately acquire temporal goods; and that the faithful would be obliged to come to the aid of the Church if it were reduced to need as a result of the depredations of the civil power.[40]

Commentators even before the Code held that if the Church should agree to comply with the civil law, it would do so not in sign of recognition that its right to acquire was derived from the civil law, but merely to give its property the protection of the civil law.[41] The guarantees provided for in the recent concordats do not, therefore, represent a departure from the traditional defense of the right to acquire, but are to be interpreted as guarantees of protection and security to be afforded by the State to church property[42].

[40] Ep. "*Acre nefariumque,*" 10 maii 1905-Fontes, n. 668.

[41] E. g., Wernz, *Ius Decretalium,* III, n. 135; Cavagnis, *Institutiones Iuris Publici Ecclesiastici,* III, n. 394.

[42] Goodwine, pp. 96-98. This explanation of the terminology in some recent con-

The basic argument in favor of the Church's right to acquire property comes from divine law. Because Christ founded the Church as a perfect society, it has the right to acquire property. Its right to acquire property is based on its social character. A visible society, composed of human beings as members, who exercised an external worship, whose ministers need support, and who are called to perform acts of corporal as well as spiritual mercy, certainly cannot exist without property. Temporal goods are necessary for the very existence of such a society. Therefore, if the Catholic Church is truly a society, then it surely has the right to acquire temporal goods.[43]

That the Church is in fact a society is evident from an examination of it. The essential elements of a society are a multitude of individuals, a purpose, common means and authority.[44] Each of these elements is easily verified in the Church. It has many members; its purpose is the salvation of those members' souls; its common means is its common faith and same means of grace in the sacraments; and its authority resides in the one Supreme Pontiff. It can further be shown that Christ Himself positively determined each of these essential elements which make the Church a society. Accordingly, the Church is a society by *divine* will and its right to acquire property, therefore also comes from divine will.

Moreover, Christ established the Church as a perfect society. He gave it for its purpose man's highest possible good in the spiritual order and endowed it with all the means necessary to attain that end. Among these means are the sacraments, and the twofold power of orders and jurisdiction.

These means are temporal as well as spiritual. They imply the possession of temporal things. Thus in giving the Church these means to attain its high goal, He implicitly established its right, independent of any other society, to acquire property. To fulfill its purpose, the Church must have churches, altars, vestments, bread and wine, houses, schools, hospitals, cemeteries, tribunals and money for the support of its ministers and its other needs. It must have these things,

cordats may also serve as a key to understanding the mind of the Church, when she incorporates under the various state laws in this country. The Church is not thereby denying her natural right to property as a perfect society, but rather is seeking to protect that right with all the safeguards thus made available to her in civil law.

43 Bouscaren, p. 797; Goodwine, p. 6; Ottaviani, *Institutiones Iuris Publici Ecclesiastici* (2vols., Romae: Typis Polyglottis Vaticanis, 1947-1948, I, 199, (hereafter cited Ottaviani).

44 Ottaviani, I, 15-20.

and the right to them because it is what it is, and that by divine institution, a perfect society.[45]

One can also argue for the right of the Church to acquire property from the natural law. It can be proved from reason alone that the Church is a society, and that every society in order to exist must have property. Therefore, if a society has the right to exist, it also has the right to acquire property. Religious societies certainly have every right to exist and accordingly from natural law have the right to acquire property. Of course, this argument considers the Church simply as a human society, whereas it is in fact a divinely established one. However, the argument has value in showing that, even when considered simply as a human society, the Church has this basic right. It fails, however, to demonstrate that this right of the Church is entirely free and independent from any civil authority.[46]

Section III. Modes of Acquisition

The Church can acquire temporal goods by all just means which are allowed for other moral and physical persons by the natural or the positive law.[47] Mortmain statutes which limit this right of the Church to acquire property, either as to the amount or means of acquisition, are here rejected by the Code. The State cannot place unjust limitations on the Church's rights of acquisition. Any means of acquisition which are just for other persons, moral or physical, according to natural law or positive law, are also just for moral persons in the Church. The term *positive law* here refers to civil law.[48] Just means allowed by the natural law include occupation, labor, and accession, either natural, or industrial, or mixed. Just means allowed by civil law include contracts, last will and testament, gifts, legal succession, and prescription or adverse possession.[49]

The ownership of property belongs to that moral person which legitimately acquired it, always under the supreme authority of the authority of the Apostolic See, however.[50] The pope's supreme authority over all Church property is analogous to the right of eminent domain, and is exercised in much the same way. Before he can allow

[45] Ottaviani, I, 199; Goodwine, pp. 6-13.

[46] Ottaviani, I, 198; Goodwine, pp. 28-29.

[47] Canon 1499,§1.

[48] Bouscaren, p. 801.

[49] *Loc. cit.*

[50] Canon 1499,§2.

property of a subordinate ecclesiastical person to be transferred to another moral person in the Church or be usurped by secular authority, he must have a proportionately grave cause and must provide adequate compensation. No one under the pope can exercise this type of power over subordinates; to attempt to do so would be to perform a canonically invalid and unjust act.[51]

A competent ecclesiastical authority, however, may divide the territory of an ecclesiastical moral person. This division may be made in such a way that part of the territory of one ecclesiastical moral person is cut off and united to another ecclesiastical moral person, or a new and distinct moral person may be created by the separated territory. In the division the common goods, which were destined for the benefit of the whole territory, and all debts contracted for the entire territory are to be divided equitably and proportionately by the competent ecclesiastical authority. However, the intentions of pious founders and donors, acquired legal rights, and particular laws governing the moral person involved must be safeguarded.[52]

Although a moral person cannot be divided, its territory or property can be divided, as well as its duties and obligations. The ordinary is the competent ecclesiastical superior for the division of parishes[53] and the Holy See is the competent authority when a province, diocese, abbacy or prelacy *nullius,* vicariate or prefecture apostolic is divided.[54] However, in the division the capital of earmarked endowments or income derived from them cannot be divided, whenever such action would constitute an interference with the will of a donor or founder.[55] Similarly, acquired rights must be respected, for example, a long-term lease of common property of a territory being divided would have to be respected in making the division. Also, particular laws governing the moral person involved, such as the special constitutions of a religious institute in the division of a religious province, must be followed.[56]

When an ecclesiastical moral person ceases to exist, its property is acquired by the moral person immediately superior to it. Here

[51] Abbo-Hannan, II, 710-711.
[52] Canon 1500.
[53] Canon 1427.
[54] Canons 215, 248, 249, 1422.
[55] Abbo-Hannan II, 661.
[56] Canon 494; Cf. Bouscaren, p. 804.

again, however, the intentions of founders and donors, acquired legal rights, and particular laws governing the extinct moral person must always be respected.[57] An ecclesiastical moral person may cease to exist, because it has been suppressed by the authority which created it, or automatically after one hundred years of inactivity or virtual nonexistence.[58] However, if only one member of a collegiate moral person survives, the rights of all are united in him.[59]

The Code treats various methods whereby moral persons in the Church may acquire the temporal goods necessary to carry out their ends and purposes. For the sake of convenience these methods will be arranged into four groups for treatment here.

A. Free-will Offerings, Taxes, and Fees.

Special statutes and laudable customs of individual countries and regions are to be observed in regard to the payment of tithes and first fruits.[60] The custom of giving tithes, a tenth part of one's income or the fruits of one's lands, and the first fruits of the soil or animals, derives from Mosaic Law.[61] During the Middle Ages such payment was obligatory. The Council of Trent insisted on their payment. However, the custom has fallen into disuse in all save a very few areas in modern times. It is found more in the Eastern Church than in the Western.[62]

Private persons, both clerical and lay, are forbidden to solicit funds for any charitable or ecclesiastical institution or purpose without the written permission of the Apostolic See or their proper ordinary and the ordinary of the place in which the collection is to be made.[63] This restriction, however, does not prohibit members of mendicant orders from making collections within the diocese in which their monastery is located.[64] Bouscaren defines begging, in the strict sense of the word, as going from door to door asking for alms for some pious purpose. "This would include seeking information regarding the names of generous persons in a certain locality, making a list of them, and then calling upon them with a re-

[57] Canon 1501.
[58] Canons 102, 699.
[59] Canon 102,§2.
[60] Canon 1502.
[61] Deut. 14:22; Num. 18:19.
[62] Bouscaren, pp. 804-805; Woywod, II, 191.
[63] Canon 1503.
[64] Canons 621-624.

quest for alms." He excludes asking help discretely from personal acquaintances, collecting alms in a church or at a meeting, visiting particular homes at the occupants' invitation, and visiting benefactors to thank them for previous gifts. Begging letters would not come under the strict demands of this law, and are allowed by custom.[65] The law speaks of private persons, that is, persons who have no special office which would entitle them to seek alms. For example, a pastor by reason of his very office, has both the right and duty to solicit alms for the various needs of the parish, and would not be considered a private person when collecting for such purposes.[66]

The *cathedraticum* is a moderate tax paid annually to the bishop by all churches and benefices subject to his jurisdiction and by all lay confraternities as well, as a token of submission to him. The amount of the tax, unless it has already been established by long-standing custom, should be determined by a provincial council of the bishops according to the regulations of canon 1507,§1.[67] The *cathedraticum* is not to vary from parish to parish, but is to be assessed identically on all or none. In Spain and Italy, as early as the sixth century, it was customary to give the bishop two *solidi* in honor of the episcopal see on the occasion of his visitation. The amount is expected to be small, as it is merely a token of submission, and should not vary from year to year.[68] During the vacancy of a diocese, the *cathedraticum* does not have to be paid to the diocesan administrator. Furthermore, a bishop does not have to insist that a *cathedraticum* be paid to him, but he can order it to be begun, if it does not exist in his diocese, in which case the amount must be that determined at the provincial council and approved by the Apostolic See.[69]

In the United States a special method of a proportionate assessment on the parishes is the usual means employed for the support of the bishop and the diocesan curia. This tax is commonly referred to as the *cathedraticum.* This, of course, is incorrect nomenclature, since the *cathedraticum* actually is not a means of support, but a small token of submission, and is not proportionate to income, but identical for all parishes. This assessment for the support of the

65 Bouscaren, p. 805.

66 *Ibid.,* p. 806.

67 Canon 1507; Cf. *infra.,* p. 63.

68 AAS, XII (1920), 444: Bouscaren, *The Canon Law Digest* (4 vols., Milwaukee: Bruce and Company, 1943-1958), I, 719 (hereafter cited Digest).

69 Bouscaren, pp. 806-807; Cf. Canons 1504 and 1507,§1.

bishop and the curia is rather a special tax, not to be confused with the *cathedraticum.*

There is some difficulty involved in reconciling this special assessment with the Code. Special taxes are treated in canons 1505 and 1506. Canon 1505 holds that, to meet some special need in the diocese, the bishop may impose a small extraordinary tax on all beneficiaries, religious as well as secular; this tax is permitted besides the seminary tax, allowed in canons 1355-1356, and the pension placed on benefices according to the norms of canon 1429. Canon 1506 adds that the only other time at which the bishop can exact a tax on churches, benefices, and other ecclesiastical institutions subject to him is at the time of foundation or consecration. This canon adds that no tax may be imposed on Mass stipends, whether manual or founded.

These canons seem to legislate against the custom in this country of placing a tax on the various parishes of the diocese, in proportion to their income, for the support of the bishop and the work of the diocesan curia. This practice stems from the legislation of the Second Plenary Council of Baltimore (1866), which directs that in order to provide for the support of the bishop, "who bears the burden and care of all," the priests having the care of souls should, in a diocesan Synod, agree on a certain sum to be given to the bishop annually. This sum is to be derived from a definite portion of the income of each church. When the sum and division has been approved by the bishop, it should be published as the law of the diocese and observed by all.[70]

This decree was approved by the Sacred Congregation for the Propagation of the Faith, the congregation under whose jurisdiction this country was at the time. The sacred congregation called for no change in the decree. When the United States came under the jurisdiction of the Sacred Consistorial Congregation in 1908, this provision was contrary to the common law to which the Church then became subject. However, the Holy See approved it as the only practical method available to meet the needs of the dioceses in this country. Further, in 1929 the Sacred Congregation for the Eastern Church approved the same method of proportioned parish assessments for

[70] *Concilii Plenarii Baltimorensis II in Ecclesia Metropelitana Baltimorensis a die VII ad diem XXI Octobris A.D. MDCCLXVI habit: et a Sede Apostolica Recogniti Acta et Decreta* (2. ed., Baltimore: John Murphy, 1880), n. 100.

the Greek-Ruthenian dioceses in the United States.[71] Accordingly, there is ample evidence that this method may be employed in the United States, although contrary to the general law, until such time as the Holy See expressly forbids it.[72] Apart from the norms of canon 1056 and 1234, it belongs to a provincial council or a meeting of the bishops of a province to determine the fees payable in the entire ecclesiastical province for the various acts of voluntary jurisdiction, for the execution of rescripts of the Apostolic See, and on the occasion of the administration of the sacraments or sacramentals. This determination of fees, however, has no force until it has been first approved by the Holy See.[73] Fees for judicial acts will be fixed according to canon 1909. Bouscaren writes that "A tax may be defined as a fee (gratuity, remuneration) imposed by canon law to be given by the faithful to the curia or to the sacred ministers on the occasion of favors granted or of the sacred ministry exercised in their favor.[74] These stole fees and curial and judicial charges must be exacted with the greatest discretion, lest the faithful misunderstand their nature and purpose. Accordingly, the law determines that they should be worked out by all the bishops of the province and thus kept uniform throughout that entire, large area. Canon 1056 permits the Ordinary to charge a small fee for matrimonial dispensations to defray chancery expenses. Canon 1234 allows the Ordinary, with the advice of the board of consultors, to determine funeral fees. Canon 1909 demands that judicial fees be determined by the bishops of the province, but does not require the subsequent approval of the Holy See.

B. Prescription.

Another mode of acquisition of temporal goods allowed in the Code is prescription. In general, the Church adopts the civil law of the individual nations in regard to prescription of ecclesiastical goods, modified, however, by the regulations of canons 1509-1512.[75]

[71] AAS, XXI (1929). 154, art. 7; *Digest,* I, 9.

[72] Bouscaren, p. 808; Cf. also, Warnz, III, N. 223; Ayrinhac, *Administrative Legislation in the New Code of Canon Law* (London). Kremer, *Church Support in the United States,* The Catholic University of America Canon Law Studies, n. 61 (Washington, D. C.: The Catholic University of America, 1930), p. 124. A contrary view is held by Abbo-Hannan, II, 713, footnote 16, and Vermeersch-Creusen, II, n. 826.

[73] Canon 1507.

[74] p. 809.

[75] Canon 1508.

Prescription is a method of acquiring the ownership of property by possessing it for a certain length of time under particular conditions laid down in law. The prescription of corporeal property in the United States is called adverse possession. Prescription, besides being acquisitive, may be liberative or exstinctive, when it is used to free one's self from an obligation by applying a statute of limitations. Conditions usually required for prescription to take place are these: a thing that is prescriptible; actual possession; some kind of title; passage of the time required by law; good faith.[76]

Generally all temporal goods, corporeal and incorporeal, movable and immovable, public and private, are prescriptible. However, positive law may remove some things from the category of prescriptible goods. The law may prohibit the prescription of some things absolutely, others relatively, that is, only at certain times or by certain classes of persons.

Thus the Church differs from civil law on prescription by classing cèrtain items as not prescriptible, some absolutely, others relatively. The Code decrees that the following goods and rights are not subject to prescription:

(1) Whatever pertains to the divine natural or divine positive law, such as property seized by theft or the primacy of the pope;

(2) Those things which can be obtained only by Apostolic privilege, such as the privilege sometimes granted to priests to administer confirmation;

(3) Spiritual rights which laymen are incapable of acquiring, when there is question of prescription in favor of laymen, as receiving a benefice or ecclesiastical jurisdiction;

(4) The certain and undisputed boundary lines of ecclesiastical provinces, dioceses, parishes, vicariates and prefectures apostolic, abbacies and prelacies *nullius;*

(5) Mass stipends and their obligations;

(6) Ecclesiastical benefices without title, although color of title suffices;

(7) The right of visitation and obedience, if the consequence would be that the subjects would thus be freed from visitation by any prelate and would no longer be subject to any prelate;

[76] Bouscaren, p. 810; Abbo-Hannan, II, 716.

(8) Payment of the *cathedraticum*.[77]

Sacred things are subject to a limited prescription. Sacred things which are owned by private persons may be prescribed by private persons, but they may not be put to profane uses. However, sacred things which have lost their consecration or blessing may be freely acquired and put to profane but not sordid uses.[78] A sacred thing loses its consecration or blessing, when it has been so badly damaged or changed that it has lost its original form and cannot be used for its original purpose. The consecration or blessing of a sacred thing is also lost, when it is used for an unbecoming purpose or when it is offered for public sale or auction.[79]

Sacred things which are not owned by a private person but by an ecclesiastical moral person may not be prescribed by a private person but only by another ecclesiastical moral person.[80]

As far as actual possession and some kind of title are concerned, the Code makes no special provisions. Accordingly, the civil law of particular places is canonized with regard to these two essential conditions of prescription. However, the Code does make special provisions in regard to the time required for prescription to occur. A period of one hundred years is required for the prescription of the following goods, if they belong to the Apostolic See: immovable things; movable, precious things; rights and claims at law, whether personal or real. If these things belong to some other ecclesiastical moral person, a period of thirty years is required for them to be acquired by prescription.[81] For all other property, belonging either to the Holy See or any other moral person in the Church, the period of time required by civil law will suffice for their prescription.

The Code also differs from the civil law with regard to the condition of good faith for prescription. Bouscaren defines good faith as: "A judgement by which one prudently concludes that he justly possesses a thing as his own without any violation of the rights of another. In the strict sense, it is a judgment of *ownership* justly acquired; in the broad sense, it is the persuasion of lawful *possession*.

[77] Canon 1509; Cf. Bouscaren, p. 718; Abbo-Hannan, II, 810-811; Woywod, II, 193-195.

[78] Canon 1510,§1.

[79] Canon 1305.

[80] Canon 1510,§2.

[81] Canon 1511.

Theologically and canonically speaking, possession of a thing which is lawful in conscience, inasmuch as it excludes sin, is sufficient to establish good faith."[82] No prescription is valid unless it is based on good faith, not only at the moment of entering into possession, but throughout the entire period required for prescription.[83]

The Code here is merely declaring a requirement of natural law. When a person keeps something which he knows belongs to another, he sins. To allow him to prescribe the thing by this means would be to reward sin, something which no law can do, civil or ecclesiastical. However, good faith is a matter of the internal forum. Accordingly, civil law for the sake of the common good may not require good faith in the external forum but may allow each individual to follow his own conscience in the matter. The Church, on the other hand, can speak freely about matters affecting the internal forum and the conscience of her subjects, and is more explicit in regard to good faith for prescription than is the civil law.[84]

Good faith must be present not only at the beginning of the possession of the thing, but throughout the full time of possession. However, an insoluable doubt, which may arise as to whether the thing may belong to someone else, does not destroy good faith or hinder prescription, provided, of course, that serious efforts to solve the doubt were made. The principle, "*in dubio melior est conditio possidentis*," may be applied to this situation.[85]

Good faith of moral persons is determined by the judgment of the person or persons who act in the name of the moral person, as, for example, the trustees of an aggregate corporation or that person who is a corporation sole.

C. Gifts and Bequests.

Any person who is entitled by the natural law and the ecclesiastical law to dispose of his goods freely may give them to pious causes, either by an act *inter vivos* or by an act *mortis causa*.[86] A common way for the Church to acquire property is through gifts and bequests for pious causes. A pious cause includes all those things which are done for a supernatural end, either by reason of the thing's direct

[82] p. 812.

[83] Canon 1512.

[84] Bouscaren, p. 812; Woywod, II, 197.

[85] Bouscaren, p. 813.

[86] Canon 1513,§1.

purpose or by reason of the intention of the donor. Supernatural ends might include the worship of God, honor of the saints, the spiritual welfare of one's neighbor, and also his temporal welfare so long as the motive is one of Christian charity and not mere philanthropy. The celebration of Mass, administration of the sacraments, building and maintenance of churches, schools, hospitals, etc., the promotion of confraternities and groups dedicated to the development of the faith and good morals among youth, are all works with a supernatural end and therefore qualify as pious causes. A purely theatrical or athletic work or association, or the building of hospitals and schools for purely philanthropic motives would exclude a supernatural end and would not qualify as pious causes. However, if a donor is a Catholic, the presumption is that his motive was more than philanthropic, being based on Christian charity, and that his gift therefore is to a pious cause.

The Code states that the donor must be a person who is allowed by natural and ecclesiastical law to dispose of his goods freely. Natural law prevents infants, the insane, persons under the influence of strong drink or drugs, and persons acting under the influence of grave and unjust fear, from the free disposal of their goods, because they are acting without the free use of their reason. Ecclesiastical law bars novices from giving away their property during their novitiate,[87] and professed religious in congregations during their lifetime.[88] However, novices in congregations must make a will before taking first vows, and religious professed of simple vows must give away all their property within the sixty-day period which immediately precedes their profession of solemn vows.[89]

In last wills made in favor of the Church, all the formalities of the civil law should be observed as far as possible; if, however, these formalities were omitted, the heirs should be admonished to fulfill the will of the testator.[90] Either a written document or the testimony of two or three reliable witnesses is enough to prove the will of the testator.[91] The word *admonished* in this law actually implies a precept. The heirs, therefore, are more than exhorted to fulfill the will of the testator, when the will is civilly invalid because of

[87] Canon 568.

[88] Canon 583,§1.

[89] Canons 569,§3 and 581,§1.

[90] Canon 1513,§2.

[91] Canon 1791,§2.

the lack of some formality; they have an obligation in conscience to carry out the provisions of the will regarding any bequest to a pious cause.[92] However, it is commonly held by canonists that necessary heirs, that is, heirs who by reason of civil law may not be excluded from at least a partial inheritance, may claim the portion to which they are entitled even against a pious cause.[93]

A last will is one of the two methods by which something may be given to a pious cause through an act *mortis causa.* An act *mortis causa* may also take the form of a donation in consideration of death. In both forms the gift is subject to revocation on the part of the donor at any time before his death, and the property is not transferred to the beneficiary until after the death of the donor. However, in a last will and testament the beneficiary need not accept the gift or even know about it for it to take effect, whereas, in a donation in consideration of death the beneficiary must accept the gift to give it effect, even though its ownership is not transferred to him by that acceptance but only after the death of the donor.

The Church may also acquire property, of course, through acts *inter vivos,* that is, any donation or other contract by which the ownership of goods is transferred to another for a pious cause. Such a transfer is irrevocable and becomes effective as soon as the beneficiary accepts it.[94]

The wishes of the faithful who give their goods to pious causes, either by an act *inter vivos* or by an act *mortis causa,* shall be executed most faithfully, even in the manner of administering and spending the gifts. However, the rights of the ordinary, as specified in canon 1515, must be safeguarded.[95] A wish of the donor as regards the manner of administration could include a restriction concerning the investment of the money or property which he is giving to the pious cause, or could be a prescription that one of his heirs serve as one of the administrators of the pious bequests. A wish of the donor as regards the manner of spending could be a limitation fixing a definite amount of money or a specific piece of property, naming a particular group (e. g., a scholarship for the boys of a particular parish), or regarding time (e. g., Masses to be said on

92 *AAS,* XXII (1930), 196; *Digest,* I, 725.

93 Bouscaren, p. 817.

94 Bouscaren, p. 814.

95 Canon 1514. Cf. *infra* p. 70.

particular days). These wishes are to be carried out most faithfully in all their details, even if other uses of the gift may seem more useful. Of course, the Holy See could allow a change in these wishes by virtue of its power of eminent domain, provided there is a sufficient cause, but an ordinary could make such a change only if he had special delegation to do so from the Holy See.[96]

Any reduction, restriction, or change of last wills is reserved to the Holy See unless the testator expressly grants this power to the local ordinary. No change may be made except for a just and necessary cause.[97] Reduction refers to a reduction in the number of acts, e. g., the number of scholarships to be awarded. Restriction refers to a more specific determination, such as restricting Masses to be offered to only sung Masses. Change or commutation refers to a substitution of one obligation for another, as devoting money left to decorate a church towards a new addition to it. A just and necessary cause is required to make any of these changes. However, a necessary cause does not mean that before a change can be made the purpose must be absolutely impossible of fulfillment. Moral impossibility is sufficient; a decidedly greater utility of the change could be considered a just and necessary cause.[98]

If fulfillment of the imposed obligations has become impossible because the revenue has become diminished or for some other reason, through no fault of the administrator, the local ordinary may diminish the obligations equitably, as long as he consults the interested parties and carries out the wishes of the testator as far as possible. However, the reduction of Masses is always reserved to the Holy See exclusively.[99] However, if the charter or articles of the foundation expressly gives him the right, the ordinary can reduce the Mass obligations.[100] Actually, ordinaries are delegated the power to reduce Mass obligations by the Holy See in their quinquennial faculties.[101]

Ordinaries are the executors of all pious wills, both *inter vivos* and *mortis causa.* In vitue of this right, the ordinary can and must exercise vigilance, even by visitation, in seeing to it that the wishes

96 *AAS,* XX (1927), 363; *Digest,* I, 724; Bouscaren, pp. 817-818.

97 Canon 1517, §1.

98 Bouscaren, p. 819-820; Abbo-Hannan, II, 723.

99 Canon 1517, §2.

100 *AAS,* XIV (1922), 529; *Digest,* I. 726.

101 *Digest,* II, 35.

of the donors are carried out. Delegated executors must give an account to the ordinary, after they have completed their task. Any clause inserted into a last will, which is contrary to this right of ordinaries, is to be ignored as non-existent.[102]

Ordinaries in this canon refers to local ordinaries and the major religious superiors of exempt organizations. A delegated executor is one appointed by the donor or testator, or by civil law, or by the ordinary himself. These must report to the ordinary, who has the right and duty of vigilance over them in seeing that they fulfill the wishes of the donor or testator.

When a cleric religious receives property in trust to be devoted to a pious cause, either by donation or by last will and testament, he must notify the ordinary of his trust and indicate to him the nature and extent of the movable and immovable goods involved together with the obligations attached to them. If the donor expressly and absolutely forbids this, the cleric or religous may not accept the trust. The ordinary must demand that the goods received in the trust be safely invested and must see to it that the trust is carried out according to the norms laid down in canon 1515. If a religious is put in trust of goods left in favor of churches, or of the inhabitants, or of pious causes of the place or of the diocese, the ordinary meant in this canon is the local ordinary; otherwise it is the proper ordinary of the religious.[103] Parochial churches, schools, orphanges, and hospitals would be under the local ordinary's supervision, whereas churches of exempt religious and their houses of study, and the like, would be under the jurisdiction of the religious ordinary. The ordinary for non-exempt religious is the local ordinary.[104]

D. Pious Foundations.

A special mode of acquisition of property by the Church is that of pious foundations. These are really a form of gifts and bequests, but since they have their own peculiar regulations, they are here treated separately. Actually pious foundations are not common in the United States, and accordingly only a very brief survey of them will be offered here.

A pious foundation is property given to some moral person in the Church together with the obligation, imposed perpetually or for

102 Canon 1515.

103 Canon 1516.

104 Bouscaren, p. 819; Canon 198.

a long time, to use the annual income from that property for the celebration of a certain number of Masses, or the performance of some other specified ecclesiastical function, or the fulfillment of certain works of piety or charity. When a foundation has been legitimately accepted, it has the nature of a bilateral contract, *do ut facias,* binding on both parties.[105]

It is the right of the ordinary to determine the limits below which a pious foundation cannot be accepted and the proper distribution of the income from the endowment. His written consent is necessary before a moral ecclesiastical person can accept a foundation, and before giving such consent he must be sure that the moral person will be able to satisfy the obligations thus imposed, as well as obligations already held. He must also make sure that the income from the endowment corresponds to the obligations imposed. The ordinary must also see that the goods are profitable and safely invested, after consulting the parties concerned and the diocesan board of administration. In the case of pious foundations in the churches, even parochial, owned by exempt religious, these rights and duties of the ordinary refer to the religious ordinary.[106]

Foundations, even those made orally, are to be put in writing, and one copy of the agreement is to be kept in the diocesan archives and another copy in the archive of the moral person receiving the foundation. The regulations of canons 1514-1517[107] are to be observed. Also, a list of the obligations shall be prepared and kept in a safe place by the rector of the church which has the foundation. Besides the book for manual stipends, the rector shall keep another book, in which he is to enter each and every obligation, perpetual and temporary, so that an exact report can be made to the ordinary.[108]

The reduction of obligations incumbent upon pious foundations is reserved exclusively to the Holy See, unless the contrary is explicitly stated in the document of foundation. Masses, however, can never be reduced without the permission of the Holy See, as canon 1517,§2 states. An indult to reduce foundation Masses does not extend to other Masses owning under contract or to other burdens of the

105 Canon 1544.

106 Canons 1545-1547 and 1550.

107 Cf. *supra,* p. 68-70.

108 Canons 1548-1549.

109 Canon 1551.

pious foundation. A general indult to reduce the obligations of a pious foundation is to be understood in the sense that the person using the indult shall, unless the contrary is apparent, reduce obligations other than Mass obligations.[109]

Obligations imposed in a pious foundation are either perpetual or for a long time. Perpetual foundations are very seldom accepted, especially because of the great difficulty in insuring the fulfillment of the obligations incumbent upon them. There is a great discrepancy among the authors in the interpretation of the *long time* mentioned here. Some put it as low as ten years, while others say fifty years. The most common interpretation is that long time here means about forty years.[110]

Article 2. Acquisition In Nevada Law

The State of Nevada has recognized and granted its legal protection to the right of the Church to acquire property. The laws of Nevada do not say that this right of the Church is hers by nature. Indeed, since United States civil law does not recognize the juridic personality of the Church as such,[111] it must be argued that the State of Nevada considers that it gives the Church this right to acquire property. Nevada expressly grants the right in its corporation laws for churches and religious societies. However, even an unincorporated church would also have the right to acquire property under common law.

In the case of Su Lee vs. Peck it was ruled that an unincorporated joss house (church) society can take title to real estate in the State of Nevada, under the common law rule that land may be given to pious uses before there is a grantee competent to take, and that in the meantime the fee lies in abeyance and vests when the grantee exists.[112] The court in this case ruled that the donor and his grantee are estopped from asserting the joss house society's incapacity to take title to the property. Thus recognition of a church's right to acquire property, even though not incorporated under Nevada law where that power is expressly granted, was upheld by the Nevada supreme court. The court does not say, however, that the Church acquires by natural right, but under the common law.[113]

[110] Bouscaren, p. 846; Abbo-Hannan, II, 784; Woywod, II, 220; DeMeester, III, n. 1499; Vermeersch-Creusen, II, n. 865.

[111] Cf. *infra*, p. 84.

[112] Su Lee vs. Peck, 40 Nev. 20, 16 Pac. 18 (1916).

[113] Chapter I, Section I, of the *Compiled Laws of Nevada (1873)* rules that the

The corporation sole act, passed that churches might incorporate for the purposes of acquiring, holding, and disposing of property, legislates that such corporations shall have the power to "acquire and possess, by donation, gift, bequest, devise, or purchase," and also shall have the power to "receive bequests and devises for its own use or upon trusts to the same extent as natural persons may."[114]

The act for the incorporation of religious, charitable, and other associations rules that their trustees or directors "may take into their possession and custody all the temporalities of such corporation, whether given, granted, or devised, directly or indirectly, to such society or association, or to any person or persons for their use."[115]

Accordingly, churches in Nevada may acquire property by the same methods which are legally available to natural persons, that is, by gifts and donations *inter vivos,* by bequests and devises in last wills and testaments,[116] and by adverse possession. Thus, a brief survey of the Nevada legislation on each of these methods of acquisition is in order here.

Section I. Gifts

The Church relies heavily upon the free-will offerings of the faithful for the financial support necessary to carry on the purposes of the Church. These free-will offerings are obtained in the main through plate collections and through subscriptions. Such voluntary donations by the faithful will be upheld by the courts in the United States, whether they consist of money, property or services.[117] Once the donor has fully executed his gift, he will not be allowed to change his mind and recover it, nor have the courts allowed the donors to exert control over property purchased with the money which they have donated. The courts in some states have held donors liable even when they merely signed subscription papers, although generally they are held to be bound only after the church has taken some specific action on the faith of the donors' promises in the sub-

common law of England shall be the rule of decision in all Nevada courts, so far as it is not inconsistent with the constitution or laws of the United States or the laws of the Territory of Nevada.

[114] NRS. 84.050.

[115] NRS. 86.120.

[116] A bequest is generally held to mean a gift in a will of personal property, and a devise is a gift in a will of real property, Cf. In re Estate of Lewis, 39 Nev. 450, 451, 4A.L.R. 241, 159 Pac. 961 (1916).

[117] Zollman, p. 422.

scription papers.[118] The courts will not excuse a donor because he signed the subscription paper on a Sunday, but will construe the signature as an act of charity and thereby except it from the Sunday laws.[119] Services rendered are also voluntary gifts, just as money deposited in a collection plate is. Thus, unless some specific evidence to the contrary is produced, courts have been accustomed to hold various services, as playing the organ, handling and investing funds, legal services rendered trustees, as free-will offerings of the faithful.[120]

Another mode of acquisition by donations *inter vivos* is the nontestamentary trust, that is, a trust created otherwise than by a will. A nontestamentary trust may be created whereby the Church is beneficiary and either some cleric or layman or serveral of them are named trustee (s). Such a trust may also be created in which the incorporated Church is the trustee and some specifically named group the beneficiaries, as, for example, the Roman Catholic Bishop of Reno, a Corporation Sole, could be named trustee to hold property the income from which is to be used to help the poor of St. Therese's parish. Again, such a trust could make little or no distinction between the trustee and the beneficiary, as property given to the Roman Catholic Bishop of Reno for the general needs of the diocese.

In this third type of trust, where trustee and beneficiary are not sufficiently distinguished, it is possible that Nevada courts would hold that these are not true trusts but outright gifts on account of the identity of trustee and beneficiary. Although there is no case history in Nevada jurisprudence to make such a conclusion, there is the precedent of other states. Some jurisdictions have held in these cases that only legal title to the property was transferred to the corporation as trustee, while other jurisdictions have held that such gifts lacked the character of technical trusts.[121] New York courts have

[118] Cf. First Universalist Society in Newburyport vs. Currier, 44 Mass. (3 Metc.) 417 (1841); Cottage Street M.E. Church vs. Kendall, 121 Mass. 528, 23 Am. Rep. 286 (1877); Presbyterian Church of Albany vs. Cooper, 112 N.Y. 517, 20 N. E. 352, 3 L.R.A. 468, 8 Am. St. Rep. 767 (1889); Rogers vs. Galloway Female College, 64 Ark. 627, 636, 637, 44 S.W. 454, 39 L.R.A. 636 (1898); Barnes vs. Perine, 12 N. Y. 18 (1854).

[119] First M. E. Church of Ft. Madison vs. Donnell, 110 Iowa 5, 81 N.W. 171, 46 L.R.A. 858 (1899); Allen vs. Duffie, 43 Mich. 1, 4 N.W. 427, 38 Am. Rep. 159 (1880); Dale vs. Knepp, 98 Pa. 389, 38 Am. Rep. 165 (1881).

[120] Zollman, p. 412. For a more complete review of Anglo-American jurisprudence on voluntary donations by the faithful, see Zollman, pp. 411-422. Nevada courts have made no specific rulings on this question. The smallness of Nevada's population is the prime cause for the small number of court rulings.

[121] Byrne, *Investment of Church Funds,* The Catholic University of America Canon

held that where the estate of the trustee and that of the beneficiary merge in one identity, the trust is extinguished and the trustee-beneficiary takes the estate.[122]

When the corporation sole is made the trustee, the ordinary himself holds that capacity. He may, however, delegate others to administer the trust in his name, and they must report to him according to the norms of canon 1515.[123] The wishes of the donor must be carried out as nearly as possible. The state may employ its *cy pres* power, when certain intentions of the donor cannot be fulfilled. Thus both canon and civil law are most careful to protect the wishes of donors. In Nevada no corporate trustee can loan trust funds to itself or an affiliate, nor to any director, officer, or employee of itself or of an affiliate, unless it pays the interest on the loan required by statute.[124] Neither can a corporate trustee directly or indirectly buy from or sell to itself any property for the trust except with the approval of the proper district court.[125] The powers of the trustee are always construed in Nevada to be attached to the office and not personal, unless the contrary is stated in the trust instrument or some amendment to it.[126] In charitable trusts in Nevada the representative of the beneficiaries who are indeterminate by the nature of the trust is the attorney general. Thus when notification of the filing of intermediary, final, or distribution accounts with the clerk of the district court is to be made to each beneficiary, the trustee must make this notification to the attorney general.[127] A trustee may be sued in his representative capacity, when he has made a contract. In this case the plaintiff must notify both the corporation which is the beneficiary and the attorney general of the existence and nature of the action, when the trust is a charitable one.[128] In nontestamentary trusts, the trustee does not have to file intermediary, final, or distribution ac-

Law Studies, n. 309 (Washington, D.C.: The Catholic University of America Press, 1951), p. 166 (hereafter cited Byrne).

122 Sheman vs. Richmond Hose Co., 230 N.Y. 462, 130 N.E. 613 (1921); Murphy, pp. 148-152, points out that in these cases the courts have exercised their *cy pres* power in order to protect the benevolent purpose of the donor.

123 Cf. *supra*, p. 68-71.

124 NRS. 163.030-163.040.

125 NRS. 163.050.

126 NRS. 163.100.

127 NRS. 165.230.

128 NRS. 163.120.

counts with the clerk of the district court, unless the settlor expressly declared so in the instrument creating the trust.[129]

Section II. Wills

Another common method by which the Church acquires property is through gifts in wills. The corporation sole act expressly gives churches so incorporated the power to receive bequests and devises. The act for the incorporation of religious, charitable and other associations speaks of temporalities which have been devised but does not expressly mention those which were bequested.[130] However, this act also uses the words given, and granted, and bequests of personal property would surely be intended to be allowed by these general terms.

Nevada law requires for the validity of wills, other than nuncupative and holographic wills, that they be in writing, signed by the testator, or by some person in his presence and by his express direction, and attested by at least two competent witnesses, who must subscribe their names to the will in the presence of the testator.[131] It is also allowed for another person to steady the hand of the testator, when he signs the will.[132] Whenever any beneficial devise, legacy, or gift is made or given to one of the subscribing witnesses to the will, the will is void unless at least two other competent witnesses sign the will.[133] In Nevada any person may make a last will and testament, provided he or she is over 18 and of sound mind, and such will is chargeable with payment of the testator's debts.[134]

Holographic wills, that is a will written entirely by the hand of the testator himself, are subject to no other form. They may be made in or out of the state of Nevada, and need not be witnessed.[135] Nuncupative or verbal wills, however, are valid in Nevada only when the estate bequeathed does not exceed $1,000 in value. For the validity of nuncupative wills, the following conditions are also required: (1) The will must be proved by two witnesses who were present at

[129] NRS. 165.160.

[130] NRS. 86.120.

[131] NRS. 133.040. Cf. Estate of Stickmoth, 7 Nev. 223 (1871).

[132] In re Gordon's Estate, 40 Nev. 300, 303, 161 Pac. 717 (1916).

[133] NRS. 133.060; In re Estate of Lewis, 39 Nev. 450, 451, 4 A.L.R. 241, 159 Pac. 961 (1916).

[134] NRS. 133.020; Cf. Abel vs. Hitt, 30 Nev. 93, 93 Pac. 227 (1908), where evidence was held showing that a testatrix was mentally incompetent to execute a will.

[135] NRS. 133.090; Hunt vs. Hunt, 11 Nev. 442 (1876).

the time it was made; (2) It must be proved that the testator, at the time of pronouncing the will, bade someone present to bear witness that such was his will, or uttered words of similar import; (3) The will must have been made at the time of the last sickness of the deceased.[136] Further, proof of a nuncupative will must be offered within six months after the testamentary words were spoken, and the words themselves or their substance must be reduced to writing within thirty days after they were spoken. This writing must be filed with the petition for the probate of the will.[137]

Any person who has a will in his possession is required in Nevada law to deliver it to the clerk of the proper district court or to the person who is named its executor in the will. He must do this within thirty days after learning of the death of the testator. The executor of a will must present the will to the district court, if he is in possession of it, within thirty days after the death of the testator or within thirty days after his learning that he has been named the executor. Neglect to make such delivery on the part of the executor without reasonable cause leaves him liable for any damages which may come to interested parties on account of his neglect.[138] A person cannot be an executor of a will in Nevada if he is under the age of his majority, convicted of a felony, or judged to be incompetent by the court by reason of drunkenness, improvidence, or want of integrity or understanding.[139] The same things disqualify a person from serving as the administrator of a will.[140] It will be remembered that in canon law the ordinary is the executor of all pious wills, as he is of all pious gifts *inter vivos,* and clauses inserted into wills contrary to this provision are to be ignored. The executor named by the testator, then, would be considered a delegated executor in canon 1515, as would an administrator named by the court, and would be obliged to report to the ordinary and act under his vigilance and right of visitation.[141] The ordinary as executor, or one delegated by him would have to comply with the civil statutes requiring delivery of the will to the proper district court. The proper district court is the one in the county where the testator was resident at the time of

136 NRS. 133.100.
137 NRS. 136.080.
138 NRS. 136.050.
139 NRS. 138.020.
140 NRS. 139.010.
141 Cf. *supra,* p. 70.

his death, or, if the testator was a non-resident, in the county where the estate is situated. If the estate is located in several counties, then the proper court is in the county where first application is made.[142]

Every devise of land in any will is construed in Nevada to convey all the estate of the devisor therein which he could lawfully devise, unless it is apparent from the wording of the will that the devisor intended to convey a less estate. Any estate, right, or interest in lands, which the testator has acquired after making his will, may pass in the same manner as if it were passed at the time of the making of the will, if it appears from the wording of the will that such is the wish of the testator.[143]

In testamentary trusts, the regulations of the Uniform Trustees' Accounting Act of 1941 would have to be followed by the ordinary, when the corporation sole has been named trustee in such a will. This act expressely states that it refers to charitable trusts.[144] This act requires the trustee to submit an itemized inventory under oath of all property of the trust to the district court within thirty days after it is his duty to take possession of the trust property. Detailed accounts of the administration of the trust property must also be filed in the district court annually by the trustee. Final and distribution accounts are also required to be submitted by the trustee. Beneficiaries must be notified of these filings. In the case of charitable trusts, the ordinary, as trustee, would notify the attorney general instead of any beneficaries. The act allows a beneficiary, who is of full age and of sound mind, to excuse the trustee as to such beneficiary from the duties imposed upon him by the act or to exempt him from liability for failure to perform those duties. Whether the attorney general could excuse the ordinary from these duties, in the case of a charitable trust in which he is the trustee, is not clear from the wording of the law. However, in the absence of any court interpretation it seems that, since the attorney general takes the place of the beneficiaries of charitable trusts in all other matters in this act, he could also represent them in this excuse or exemption.[145]

[142] NRS. 136.010.

[143] NRS. 133.210-133.220; In re Estate of Lewis, 39 Nev. 450, 451, 4 A.L.R. 241, 159 Pac. 961 (1916). A married woman can lawfully devise without consent only her separate property; community property can be devised only by application of the particular laws for community property. Cf. NRS. 144.060-144.130.

[144] NRS. 165-230.

[145] Cf. Chapter 163 of *Nevada Revised Statutes* for full details of the Uniform Trustees' Accounting Act.

Section III. Adverse Possession

Adverse possession in American Law may be defined as "the enjoyment of land, or such estate as lies in grant, under such circumstances as indicate that such enjoyment has been commenced and continued under an assertion or color of right on the part of the possessor."[146] Prescription in American Law is "a mode of acquiring title to incorporeal hereditaments by immemorial or long-continued enjoyment."[147] A limitation of actions in American Law refers to "the restriction by statute of the right of action to certain periods of time, after the accruing of the cause of action, beyond which, except in certain specified cases, it will not be allowed. Also the period of time so limited by law for the bringing of actions."[148] All three of these entities in American Law, adverse possession, prescription, and limitation of actions, are included in the *praescriptio* of canon law.[149] That which is of primary concern in this work is only adverse possession, since the real property of the Church can be acquired by the adverse possession of it according to the norms of civil law. This means of acquisition has been most important to religious societies, because the proof or validity of deeds and wills by which they have held property has often been unable to stand up in American courts. Without the statutes of adverse possession, then, much of this property could have easily been lost by these churches, causing irreparable harm and injustice.[150]

The time required in Nevada law for adverse possession to be constituted is five years.[151] Canon law requires the passage of one hundred years for the prescription of immovable things, movable precious things, and real or personal rights and claims at law, when these things belong to the Apostolic See, and the passage of thirty years for the prescription of the same things when they belong to some other moral person in the Church.[152]The time required for the prescription or adverse possession of all other things is left to the

[146] Martin, *Adverse Possession, Prescription and Limitation of Actions. The Canonical "Praescriptio"*, The Catholic University of America Canon Law Studies, n. 202 (Washington, D.C.: The Catholic University of America Press, 1944), p. 4 (hereafter cited Martin).

[147] *Loc. cit.*

[148] Black, *Black's Law Dictionary* (St. Paul, Minn., West Publishing Co., 1933), p. 1119 (hereafter cited *Black's Law Dictionary*).

[149] Cf. *supra*, pp. 63-66.

[150] Zollman, p. 522.

[151] NRS. 11.110.

[152] Canon 1511. Cf. *supra*, p. 65.

provisions of civil law by the Code.[153] Accordingly, five years would be the time required for the adverse possession of these things in Nevada.

The Code makes no special provision regarding actual possession and some kind of title, two essential conditions for prescription, leaving the regulations concerning them to civil legislation. In Nevada the law states that whenever it appears that an occupant, or those under whom he claims, has taken possession of premises, under claim of title, exclusive of any other right, founding such claim upon a written instrument as being a conveyance of the premises in question, or founding the claim upon the decree or judgment of a competent court, and when it also appears that there has been a continued occupation and possession of the premises or some part of such premises, under this claim, for five years, the premises so included shall be deemed to have been held adversely. However, when the premises consist of a tract of land divided into lots, the possession of one lot cannot be deemed the possession of any other lot of the same tract.[154]

Actual possession in Nevada for the purpose of constituting adverse possession by a person who claims title based on some written instrument of a judgment or decree takes place in the following instances:

(1) Where the property has been usually cultivated and improved;

(2) Where the property has been protected by a substantial inclosure;

(3) Where, though not inclosed, it has been used for the supply of fuel, or of fencing timber, for the purpose of husbandry; or for the use of pasturage, or for ordinary uses of the occupant;

(4) Where a known farm or single lot has been improved, the portion of such farm or lot which may have been left not cleared, or not inclosed according to the usual course and custom of the adjoining country, shall be deemed to have also been occupied for the same length of time as the part improved and cultivated.[155]

The conditions for adverse possession are different in Nevada, however, when there has been actual, continued possession of the

[153] Canon 1508. Cf. *supra,* p. 65.

[154] NRS. 11.110.

[155] NRS. 11.120; Cf. Gander vs. Simpson, 37 Nev. 1, 4, 137 Pac. 514 (1914);

premises, under a claim of title, exclusive of any other right, but when such claim is not founded on any written instrument, or a judgment or decree. When these are lacking, the premises so occupied, and no other, shall be deemed to have been held adversely where the property has been protected by a substantial inclosure or where it has been usually cultivated or improved. Also, it must be able to be proved that the land has actually been occupied and claimed continuously for a period of five years, and the occupant must have paid the taxes.[156]

When the claim of title is based upon a written instrument or a judgment or decree, the fact of the payment of taxes by either the mortgagor or mortgagee after the mortgage debt was due will not arrest the operation of the statute of limitations in favor of the mortgagee in possession in an action to redeem mortgaged real estate.[157] The payment of taxes seems to be important to adverse possession only when the claim to title is not based upon a written instrument or judgment or decree.

In these conditions for adverse possession, the Nevada statutes make no express mention of the necessity of good faith. However, it is well to remember, with Martin, that "Good faith, while not much discussed in the American Law, and usually said not to be required by it, is nonetheless important if one considers the requirements of the holding in adverse possession and prescription and the attitude of the law in the event of fraud."[158] In American law good faith means an honest intention to abstain from taking an unconscientious advantage of another and freedom from knowledge of any circumstances which would lead to further inquiry about the matter. Thus it protects a purchaser, holder, or creditor from being implicated in an effort by another person with whom he is dealing to defraud some party in interest.[159] Courts of equity put much weight on good faith in cases of fraud.

Good faith has a definite bearing in Nevada jurisprudence when damages are claimed for withholding property recovered, upon

O'Banion vs. Simpson, 44 Nev. 188, 189, 191 Pac. 1083 (1920).

[156] NRS. 11.130-11.150; Small vs. Robbins, 33 Nev. 304, 110 Pac. 1128 (1910). 112 Pac. 274 (1910), 125 Pac. 770 (1912); Cassinelli vs. Humphrey Supply Co., 43 Nev. 208, 183, Pac. 523 (1919).

[157] Borden vs. Clow, 21 Nev. 275, 278, 37 Am. St. Rep. 511, 30 Pac. 821 (1892).

[158] p. 168.

[159] Martin, p. 32.

which permanent improvements have been made by the defendant or by those under whom he claims. When such holding was under color of title adversely to the claims of the plaintiff, in good faith, the value of such permanent improvements shall be allowed as a set-off against the damages which were claimed.[160]

Just as canon law lists some things which are not prescriptible, such as the certain and undisputed boundary lines of parishes,[161] so civil law may remove certain things from the realm of prescription or adverse possession. Thus a Nevada statute declares that no prescriptive right to the use of water for irrigation or to public water can be acquired by the adverse possession or use of it.[162] However, civil law allows the prescription of things declared not prescriptible by the Code.

While a written instrument showing a claim to title is most important, adverse possession may be constituted without it by merely taking possession of the property and maintaining it for the required time of five years. However, only the property actually and continually possessed can be acquired. Other portions of the property, subject to adverse possession when a written instrument or a judgment or decree is used as the claim to title, cannot be acquired when there is no written instrument. Also the occupant must be able to prove to the court that he continually occupied the premises and paid taxes upon it. Since the Church is exempt from paying taxes on its property, it seems that this requirement would not be demanded in the case of adverse possession by the Church without a written instrument. However, there is no court decision in Nevada law on the point, leaving some doubt about the question.

Thus the possession of some written instrument, as a deed which is void because the grantor had no title, is of great value in giving color of title. Church property is often dated back many years and clear evidence of the Church's title to such property may not be available. Accordingly, all instruments which show the basis for the Church's claim to the property become important evidence in the Church's behalf, since such instruments, even though void, facilitate the constitution of a clear and absolute title through adverse possession.[163]

[160] NRS. 40.040.

[161] Cf. *supra*, pp. 64-65.

[162] NRS. 533.060.

[163] Cf. Zollman, pp. 522-531.

CHAPTER IV

TENURE OF CHURCH PROPERTY

ARTICLE I. MORAL PERSONALITY

Church property belongs to the moral person which legally acquired it; but it remains subject to the supreme authority of the Apostolic See.[1] The dominion or ownership of church property, or what Anglo-American law terms legal and equitable title to church property, cannot be vested in a private person; it must be vested in a moral person. Physical persons are only the administrators of church property, not the owners. A moral person has a separate and distinct existence in its own right, independent of the individuals who make up that moral person. It has rights and duties which are not the individual rights and duties of the members who constitute it.[2] Moral persons, collegiate and non-collegiate, have the status of minors.[3] Thus the law extends the same protection to moral persons as is given to minors. The moral person is represented by agents or administrators, just as a minor is represented by his parent, tutor, or guardian.[4] Likewise, a moral person enjoys the right of *restitutio in integrum,* as a minor does.[5]

While the Church itself and the Apostolic See are moral persons by divine institution, the other moral persons in the Church, dioceses, parishes, religious institutes, etc., receive their juridic personality either by provision of ecclesiastical law or by a formal decree of a competent superior.[6] It is through these moral persons, then, that the tenure of church property is provided for. Before the Code settled the question, authors differed greatly in determining where the ownership of ecclesiastical goods lay. Some held that ownership was vested in God, or Christ, or one of the saints; others claimed that dominion of church property rested in the members of a congregation; others said that the pope was the sole owner of church pro-

[1] Canon 1499, §2.

[2] Brown, *The Canonical Juristic Personality With Special Reference to its Status in the United States of America,* The Catholic University of America Cannon Law Studies. n.39 (Washington. D.C.: The Catholic University of America Press, 1927), p. 98 (hereafter cited Brown); Michiels, *Principia Generalia de Ecclesia* (2 ed. Parisilis-Tornaci-Romae: Desclee, 1955), pp. 356-357 (hereafter cited Michiels).

[3] Canon 100,§3.

[4] Cf. canons 1647-1649.

[5] Canon 1688,§1.

[6] Canon 100,§1. Cf. *supra,* p. 25; Michiels, p. 394.

perty, while some held that the dominion was vested in the poor. The Code settled the dispute by stating that church property belongs to the ecclesiastical moral person who has acquired it legitimately. The pope has supreme jurisdiction and can exercise his powers of eminent domain, as the supreme dispenser and administrator of all ecclesiastical goods, but the dominion of the property is vested in the various moral persons in the Church.[7]

Anglo-American law does not recognize the juridical personality of the Church, as such, holding that the State is the sole creator of corporations or legal personality.[8] Civil Law in the United States looks upon all corporations as creatures of the state. The Church is a pious union of the faithful for purposes of worship and charity, but is not a corporation, and has no legal personality in its own right. The State provides for the incorporation of churches under its laws, and holds that only by this means can the Church obtain legal personality. The Church, then, must go through the same procedures as any business or lay association in order to gain recognition from the State as a legal personality with all the rights and duties pursuant to such personality. This view is clearly in conflict with the claim of the Church that it has such moral personality by divine institution and that the subordinate moral persons in the Church are created as such by the Church and not by the State.

However, this conflict is more in theory than in practice. The State looks upon the Church and the corporation through which it holds its property as two distinct entities. Incorporation does not effect the purely ecclesiastical element of the Church. The corporation is created simply as a means for the management of the temporal affairs of the Church. It is meant to give the Church a more favorable status civilly than it would otherwise enjoy. It is meant as a protection for the Church. It is not intended to alter its ecclesiastical character.[9]

[7] Doheny, *Church Property: Modes of Acquisition,* The Catholic University of America Canon Law Studies, n.41 (Washington, D.C.: The Catholic University of America, 1927), pp. 37-38 (hereafter cited Doheny); canon 1518.

[8] Brown, p. 2; Blackstone, *Commentaries on the Laws of England* (4 vols., New York: 1892), I, 472. (hereafter cited Blackstone).

[9] Brown, pp. 132-134; Cf. Klix vs. Polish Roman Catholic St. Stanislaus, 137 Mo. App. 347, 118 S.W. 1171 (1909); Zollman, *American Civil Church Law,* Columbia University Studies, Vol. 77 (New York: 1917), p. 79; McGrath, "Canon Law and American Church Law: A Comparative Study," *The Jurist,* XVIII, (1958), 264-267.

Article 2. Modes Of Tenure In The United States

The Church follows the laws of the various States for civil incorporation. She does so, not as any acknowledgment that such incorporation is necessary to give her moral personality, but as a means to insure civil stability, to safeguard property, and to avoid unnecessary litigation.[10] The States have different laws for the incorporation of churches and religious societies. The most common methods in this country for holding church property are fee simple, corporation aggregate, and corporation sole.

During the nineteeth century most of the church property in the United States was held by lay trustees. However, this method proved to be unsatisfactory, as the lay trustees used their control over church goods to interfere in purely ecclesiastical matters. These abuses were condemned by Rome in 1822 and steps were taken in the first several provincial councils of Baltimore to do away with this method of holding church property. The bishops sought to incorporate, where this was possible, or to have the bishop, himself, hold the property in fee simple where corporation was not permitted. Fee simple also proved unsatisfactory since it left the ecclesiastical goods open to encumbrance by personal creditors of the bishop, and left its tenure in grave doubt when the bishop died.[11]

In 1911 the Sacred Congregation of the Council was petitioned by the American bishops to give directions for the holding of church goods in this country. After obtaining the opinions of the archbishops in the country through the apostolic delegate, the congregation laid down the following norms on July 29:

> 1. Among the methods which are now in use in the United States for holding and administering church property, the one known as *Parish Corporation* is preferable to the others, but with the conditions and safeguards which are now in use in the State of New York. The bishops therefore should immediately take steps to introduce this method for the handling of property in their dioceses, if the civil law allows it. If the civil law does not allow it, they should exert their influence with the civil authorities that it may be made legal as soon as possible.

10 Doheny, p. 38.

11 Brown, pp. 149-151.

2. Only in those places where the civil law does not recognize *Parish Corporations,* and until such recognition is obtained, the method commonly called *Corporation sole* is allowed but with the understanding that in the administration of ecclesiastical property the Bishop is to act with the advice, and in more important matters with the consent, of those who have an interest in the premises and of the diocesan consultors, this being a conscientious obligation for the bishop in person.

3. The method called in *fee simple* is to be entirely abandoned.[12]

Section I. Corporation Aggregate: The New York Plan

There is no method of holding property in United States law which is in perfect conformity with all the regulations of canon law. However, of the various modes available to the Church in this country, that called the *Parish Corporation* has been officially declared to be the most preferable. This method is a type of aggregate corporation. An aggregate corporation is defined by Brown as "a juridical person incorporating the members of a parish or congregation."[13] Various aggregate corporations, however, will differ in the manner established for the management of the corporation. The aggregate incorporation of a parish or congregation makes each individual of the parish or corporation a member of the corporation, even though the names of only a very few members are included in the articles of incorporation. Thus, *de iure,* "the sovereignty of the legal personality is referable to the members themselves."[14] However the *de facto* exercise of this sovereignty depends upon the method established for the appointment of the directors or trustees of the corporation. If all these directors are elected by a majority of the members of the parish, the laity will have actual control of the church property. If the directors or trustees are ecclesiastics, by reason of their official position, and if the naming of all directors is controlled by the church authorities, the danger of lay control of church goods is removed, and the demands of canon law are more nearly met. Without this important feature in a corporation aggre-

[12] *Digest,* II, 444-445.

[13] P. 137.

[14] *Ibid.,* p. 138.

gate, the lay members of the parish could control the goods of the parish, even if these fell into heresy or recusancy.[15] It is because the New York law for parish corporations keeps the *de facto* control of the management of the church property in the hands of the church authorities, that the sacred congregation favored that method of incorporation for all American dioceses.[16]

The New York plan provides that the archbishop or bishop, the vicar general, the pastor of the parish being incorporated, and two laymen selected by these three, may incorporate the parish by filing articles of incorporation with the secretary of state. The New York courts have interpreted this statute as having the effect of incorporating all the members of the parish, not just the five trustees who file the incorporating document with the secretary of state. The trustees have the office of managing the corporation, and the method established for their appointment insures that the incorporated parish will remain under ecclesiastical control.[17]

The New York corporation law was named as preferable by the sacred congregation because of the special "conditions and safeguards" which it contains. These concern the manner of selecting the five trustees and filling their offices when they become vacant, the requirements for the validity of the acts of these trustees, and the rules for the disposition of property in the event of the division of a parish.

With regard to the naming of the five trustees, filling vacancies in their offices, and the validity of their acts, the New York statute decrees:

> The Archbishop or Bishop, and the Vicar General of the diocese to which any incorporated Roman Catholic church belongs, the rector of such church, and their successors in office, shall, by virtue of their offices, be trustees of such church. Two laymen, members of such incorporated church, selected by such officers or a majority of them, shall also be trustees of such incorporated church, and such officers and such laymen trustees shall together constitute the board of trustees thereof. The two laymen signing the cer-

[15] Klix vs. Polish Roman Catholic St. Stanislaus, 137 Mo. App. 347,118 S.W. 1171 (1909).

[16] Cf. Brown, pp. 137-140.

[17] People's Bank vs. St. Anthony's Roman Catholic Church, 109 N.Y. 512, 17 N.E. 408 (1888).

> tificate of incorporation of an incorporated Roman Catholic church shall be the two laymen trustees thereof during the first year of its corporate existence. The term of office of the two laymen trustees of an incorporated Roman Catholic church shall be one year. Whenever the office of any such laymen trustee shall become vacant by expiration of term or otherwise, his successor shall be appointed from the members of the church, by such officers or a majority of them. No act or proceeding of the trustees of any such incorporated church shall be valid without the sanction of the Archbishop or Bishop of the diocese to which such church belongs, or in their absence or inability to act, without the sanction of the Vicar General or of the administrator of such diocese.[18]

Thus the archbishop or bishop, the vicar general, and the pastor of each parish so incorporated, are *ipso facto* members of the five-man board of trustees, giving ecclesiastics a majority of the board membership. Their successors in office become trustees as soon as they succeed to the office. Furthermore, these three board members have the power of naming the two laymen who will serve on the board of trustees with them. The laymen hold office for only one year, so that the ecclesiastics could easily replace a laymen who became a heretic or in any way fell away from the church. Finally, the bishop's authority, as supervisor of the church property in his diocese, is protected by the regulation invalidating acts of the trustees which do not have the bishop's sanction.

With regard to the division of parishes, the New York statute also gives the archbishop or bishop powers to act, which are quite consonant with the powers granted him in the Code.[19] The New York statute regarding the division of parishes reads as follows:

> Wherever a Roman Catholic parish has been heretofore or shall hereafter be duly divided by the Roman Catholic bishop having jurisdiction over said parish and the original Roman Catholic church corporation is given one part of the old parish, and a new or second Roman Catholic church corporation is given the remaining part of the old parish, and it further appears that by reason of the said division

[18] This is #91 of the *New York Religious Corporations Law.* The text, as given here, was taken from Bouscaren's *Digest,* II, 444-445.

[19] Cf. Canon 1427.

> the original Roman Catholic church corporation holds title to real property situated within the part of the old parish that was given to the new or second Roman Catholic church corporation, then the said Roman Catholic bishop or his successor shall have the right and power, of himself, independently of any action or consent on the part of the trustees of the original Roman Catholic church corporation to transfer the title of the said real property, with or without valuable consideration, to the new or second Roman Catholic church corporation. Said transfer shall be made by the said Roman Catholic bishop or his successor after having complied with the requirements of the code of civil procedure in the same manner as the trustees of any religious corporation are compelled to do before making a transfer of church property. If a valuable consideration is paid for the transfer the same shall be received by the said . . . original Roman Catholic church corporation and the new or second Roman Catholic corporation in such proportions as in the discretion of said bishop or his successor may seem proper.[20]

This power gives the bishop independent power in the matter of the division of parishes. The Code likewise gives the bishop independence in dividing parishes, so long as he acts with a just and canonical cause. The Code remarks that he may divide the parish even against the will of its rector and without the consent of the people, although recourse may be had to the Holy See *in devolutive.* The Code also calls for the division of the goods between the new and old parishes to be done by the bishop in proper proportion and in all fairness.[21] Thus the concord between the New York statute and the canons of the code is remarkable in this matter of the division of parishes.

Section II. Fee Simple

Fee Simple, that freehold estate in land through which absolute ownership of the property is held, was abolished by the sacred congregation as a means of holding church property in the United States The bishops, who resorted to this means of tenure in their

[20] *New York Religious Corporations Law,* #92, as quoted in Brown, pp. 142-143.
[21] Canons 1427, 1428, 1500.

efforts to end the abuse of lay trusteeism, found from their experience that it was a most unsatisfactory method of holding church property. Too often property held in fee simple was subject to taxation. Again the church property of a diocese held in this way could be assigned to the creditors in the event of bankruptcy. The bishop, as absolute owner in civil law, was liable for all parish debts. When the bishop died, the tenure of the church property was in a most confused state, at least until a successor to his office was named. In order to transfer the property to his successor, a will was required and it was contestable often enough at civil law and such wills were at times successfully broken. Even when proper transfer to the bishop's sucessor was made, inheritance taxes, especially burdensome on the smaller, poorer dioceses, were sometimes exacted. Also, property which had been willed to the bishop after his death was claimed by his successor only after very difficult litigation in some jurisdictions.[22]

In some States, where the corporation aggregate and corporation sole are not available to the Church, the bishop holds the property as trustee. Although this trustee tenure is not expressly endorsed by the sacred congregation, it must have implicit endorsement, since the only other method of tenure, fee simple, is expressly ordered to be abandoned. A construction of the Texas courts has made it possible for the bishops in the State to hold legal title to all church property in trust for the Catholic Church. The trust is construed by the courts in virtue of the purposes of the office of the bishop.[23] Texas courts hold that church property conveyed to any Church official in his official capacity is held by him in trust for that Church. Thus, if property should be conveyed to a pastor by reason of his office as pastor, the legal title to such property would rest in the pastor, with the equitable or beneficial title resting in the Church.[24] This system of tenure removes some of the dangers inherent in the fee simple method and is an improvement over it, although it seems to be a long way removed from an ideal mode of holding church property.

Section III. Corporation Sole

The sacred congregation did recognize the corporation sole as a legitimate method of tenure in places where the *Parish Corporation*

22 Doheny, p. 41.

23 Blanc vs. Asbury, 63 Tex. 489, 51 Am. Rep. 666 (1885); Gabert vs. Olcott, 22 S.W. 286, rev's in Olcott vs. Gabert, 23 S.W. 985 (1893).

24 Clark vs. Brown, 108 S.W. 421 (civ. App.) rev'd in Brown vs. Clark, 102

with the safeguards guaranteed by the New York statute is not available. Thus corporation sole is given approval as a secondary or alternate mode of Church tenure in the United States. It can be considered legitimate only in the event that corporation aggregate is not available. The congregation further qualifies its approval of corporation sole by the reminder that a bishop holding ecclesiastical goods in this manner is to administer such property with the advice or consent, depending upon the importance of the act, of those who have an interest in the premises and his diocesan consultors. This is an obligation in conscience for the bishop. Furthermore, the congregation declared that bishops should strive to have the civil authorities pass laws which would make the *Parish Corporation,* similar to New York's, available to them in their respective states.[25]

"A corporation sole consists of one person only and his successors in some particular station, who are incorporated by law, in order to give them some legal capacities and advantages, particularly that of perpetuity, which in their natural capacities they could not have had."[26] The American conception of the corporation sole derives from English law, where kings, bishops, vicars, etc., were granted the right of corporation sole so that property held by them in their official capacity would not pass on to their heirs when they died. A corporation sole was considered immortal. It was considered one moral person, regardless of how many incumbents held the office. "The present incumbent and his predecessors who lived seven hundred years ago are in law one and the same person, and what was given to the one was given to the others also."[27]

Brown writes that tenure of church property by corporation sole has distinct advantages in that it grants security to church holdings by making them freely descendable to each holder of the episcopal office, and also in that it allows the bishop to carry on his corporate life by applying canonical principles which will not be disturbed by the civil law. However, he writes that it is not an ideal method of tenure, "since confusion prevales as to whether such a corporation could alienate its property without the parishioners' consent, and as to whether a *cestui que trust* might have equity to compel the corporation sole to surrender its legal title to diocesan pro-

Tex. 323, 116 S.W. 360, 24 L.R.A. (N.S.) 670 (1909).

[25] Cf. *supra,* p. 85.

[26] Blackstone, I, 470.

[27] *Ibid.,* 469-470; Brown, pp. 145-146.

perty. Finally, the death of the Ordinary suspends the *de facto* corporate life of the corporation sole and thus inactivity and consequent confusion exist through the entire period of the inter-regnum."[28] However, it seems that such confusion concerning alienation is absent in the corporation sole law as passed in Nevada, in so far as the statute expressly grants the power to the corporation sole "to buy, sell, lease, mortgage, and in every way deal in real and personal property in the same manner that a natural person may, and without the order of any court."[29] Also, the question of confusion during the period of inter-regnum following the death of the bishop and before his successor takes office, can be eliminated by making express provision for this period in the articles of incorporation. Thus in the articles of incorporation for the diocese of Reno it is expressly mentioned that during this inter-regnum an administrator is named and he "takes charge of the spiritual affairs of said Diocese, and has power and authority to administer all the temporalities and all the estate and property of the said Diocese, and to function and act as the incumbent of the Corporation Sole thereof until the appointment of a new Bishop of said Diocese, or until the removal of such Administrator by the authority appointing him."[30]

Article 3. Tenure In Nevada

Section I. Applicability of Most Corporation Laws to the Church in Nevada

Among the twelve corporation acts carried in Nevada Revised Statutes, only three merit serious consideration as offering modes of tenure for the Catholic Church. None of the acts specifically excludes churches from incorporating under its provisions, but most of them by their very nature militate against such a use of them.

It is, of course, possible for the Church in Nevada to incorporate under the General Corporation Law of 1925. As a matter of fact, Brown gave special consideration to such a mode of Church incorporation, as one means through which the Church might endeavor to bring about a new and more satisfactory "era in her corporate status in the United States."[31] Under the Nevada General Cor-

[28] p. 148.

[29] NRS. 84. 050,n.3.

[30] Articles of Incorporation of the Roman Catholic Bishop of Reno, and His Successors, a Corporation Sole, as taken from a certified copy of same.

[31] p. 194.

poration Law, and under laws similar to it in the other States, the Church would incorporate as a stock corporation. Non-transferable shares of stock could be issued to the incorporators, who might be the bishop, vicar general, pastor of the church in question, and two laymen from the parish selected by the first three. It could be arranged that the bishop always held more than fifty per cent of the stock and thus maintained the control of the corporation. Also, in the articles of incorporation it could be designated that the stock could be held only by the successors in office of the five above named trustees.

Brown points out that the advantages of such a system of incorporation would be these: the fact that it could be put into practice in practically every State in the Union, thus making for a certain uniformity in Church tenure in this country; the fact that the controlling supervision over the property would be placed in the hands of the bishop, a situation which blends with the norms of the Code; the fact that in the event of the dissolution of the corporation, there would be certain identification of the members, who hold the property as trustees for the benefit of all the parishioners.

However, he points out disadvantages in the system, which far outweigh its benefits. He suggests, first of all, that the plan might be limited in practice "by the attitude of the people in the different states with regard to the coincidence of such a plan with public policy, for such a procedure under the states' incorporating laws might be looked upon by the majority of the citizens as a legal trick, which would accordingly be promptly prohibited by the different state legislatures." Secondly, he points out, the actual control of the bishop under this plan would be uncertain. Application could be made of the principle that "the director of a corporation acquires no additional authority to act for the corporation, from the fact that he owns a majority of the corporate stock."[32] It would have been held in such a case that "the stockholders of a corporation at a general meeting can not, even by a unanimous vote, bind the corporation by contract; their action would at most be advisory and not obligatory upon the directors."[33] Finally, Brown argues, " the dissolution problem would not be remedied in the event that ecclesiastical corporations were to become stock organizations, for under

[32] Clement vs. Young-McShea Amusement Co., 69 N.J. Eq. 347, 67 A.82; Allemong vs. Simmons, 124 Ind. 199, 23 N.E. 768; as quoted in Brown, p. 195.

[33] Insurance Bank of Columbus vs. Bank of the U.S., 4 Clark 125 (pa.) as quoted in Brown, p. 195.

the present plan of Church corporation, the statutes provide for reincorporation, and further if it should ever happen that the State was bent upon escheating to the civil government of the funds of the dissolved corporation, no legal device could prevent such a disposition."[34]

The Dominican Sisters of San Rafael, California, incorporated their St. Mary's Hospital in Reno under the General Corporation Law of 1903. As such, theirs is a stock corporation. Since their purpose in incorporating was broader than the conducting of a hospital (it included the establishment of education institutions as well), the hospital was not incorporated under the Hospital Act but under the general law instead. The 1903 law has been replaced by the 1925 General Corporation Act, and St. Mary's Hospital, Inc. now comes under the directives of that law.

The Cooperative Associations Act (1901), the Nonprofit Cooperative Corporations Act (1921), are all unsuitable as methods of Church incorporation in Nevada. Since these are cooperative associations, they are naturally opposed to a hierarchical society, such as the Catholic Church. Under these systems of incorporation, the big danger would be a return of something like the lay trusteeism of the last century, since the control of the bishop over the ecclesiastical goods could be greatly reduced under this type of incorporation. The Cooperative Associations Act of 1901 in particular would put the control of property back into the hands of the laity, because this act expressly states that the rights and interest of all members is to be equal. Also, these acts all call for the formation or corporations which are temporary, not to exceed fifty years before dissolution. The Church must be considered as a perpetual corporation, not one able to be dissolved by the expiration of its charter.

Another act which is clearly not intended for use by Churches for incorporation is the one providing for the formation of Nonprofit Corporations for Advancement of State and Local Interests (1949). The purposes of a Church corporation are and must be religious and charitable. The purposes of these corporations are public and civic in nature. The inadequacy of this act for Church incorporation is obvious and needs no further development.

Similarly, the very purposes of the act providing for the formation of corporations by gymnastic, athletic, historic, scientific, and

[34] Brown, p. 195.

literary societies (1865) do not include the purposes of the Church and therefore could not be considered as a method for Church incorporation in Nevada. It is true that some Catholic societies of lay people, such as Catholic Youth Organization, Newman Club, etc., might wish to become incorporated under this act. However, these societies are not moral persons in the Church and their property, therefore, is not ecclesiastical goods.[35] But the diocese itself could not incorporate under this act.

Although cemeteries are a legitimate part of Church property, there would be no reason for the Church to incorporate its cemeteries under the Cemetery Associations Act (1865). The Church would wish to control cemetery property in the same way as all other ecclesiastical property is controlled, not under a separate corporation law. Also, in as much as this act calls for an association on a more or less equal basis, it may be argued that it does not fit with the canonical provision of ecclesiastical control over such property. The act provides that the directors of the association should be elected for terms of one, two, and three years. Thus, the bishop would have to be elected at least every three years just to be a member of the board of administrators. If all the members of a parish were considered as members of the cemetery association, they would have control of the property. If only a few persons, primarily ecclesiastics, formed the association, there would be great difficulty in keeping the property under Church control after their deaths, since the act provides no method of succeeding to trusteeship or even membership in the association by virtue of one's office.

The act which provided for the incorporation of hospitals and charitable asylums has been employed by the Dominican Sisters of Adrian, Michigan, for the incorporation of Rose De Lima Hospital in Henderson, Nevada. This act allows hospitals to hold real and personal property, which they may take and receive by gift, grant, devise, or bequest. The property may be held, however, only for those purposes for which the corporation was formed. They may not hold lands for more than ten years, except those lands which are necessary for the direct and reasonable use or convenience of the hospital. Their trustees must be at least three and no more than fifteen. Rules for their election, term of office, mode of appointment of successors, etc., is to be provided for in the articles of in-

[35] Cf. *supra*, p. 49.

corporation. They are required to make a report to the county commissioners in the county where their hospitals are located annually, and biannually to the legislature. They may invest their funds by loan, on mortgaged security, or by purchase of any city, county, state, or United States bonds, or by loan on pledge of the same. Thus there are certain limitations placed on the Sisters when they so incorporate, but sufficient freedom seems to be allowed them to carry on their charitable work in their own ways and according to the particular regulations of their religious institute.

Another act which may be eliminated from consideration as a means of Church incorporation is the Charitable and Eleemosynary Corporation Act (1945). One of the basic purposes of the Church is works of charity. It might even be construed that in Nevada civil law charitable and religious purposes are sufficiently synonymous to allow the Church to consider this act as intended for its incorporation.[36] However, even if it were considered suitable to use this act for the incorporation of a church, the act itself contains provisions which make it unsatisfactory for the Catholic Church's incorporation. On the favorable side it would be possible under this act to determine that the trustees were to be the bishop, vicar general, pastor, or any other arrangement which would be consonant with canon law. The act leaves it for the corporation to determine, in its articles of incorporation, the number of trustees (at least three), the manner by which they are to chosen, and their term of office. Thus certain trustees could be determined by the ecclesiastical office itself, as the episcopal office. However, the act declares that no funds or property may be held by the corporation for any purpose other than a charitable or eleemosynary one. This would leave some uncertainty. If a court should decide that *charitable* and *religious* are not here synonymous, much of the property of the Church could be taken away from it. Furthermore, the act declares that no member of the board of trustees may receive any compensation. However, one of the purposes of ecclesiastical goods is the support of the clergy. These would be members of the board of trustees, and accordingly, it would be unlawful for them to support themselves from Church funds, if the Church incorporated under this law.

Elimination of these corporation acts leaves only two acts in Nevada law which deserve serious consideration as methods for

[36] Cf. Nixon vs. Brown, 46, Nev. 439, 214 Pac. 524 (1923), where widest and most liberal interpretation of the term charity is called for; also, NRS. 361.140, where

Church incorporation. Both of these acts were written primarily for churches. One is the corporation sole act (1915), and the other is the act which provides for the corporation of religious, charitable, literary, scientific, and other associations (1867).

Section II. Application of Nevada's Corporation Sole Act

The Catholic Church in Nevada has actually incorporated under the corporation sole act. Upon the creation of the diocese of Reno in 1931, Bishop Thomas Gorman, first bishop of the new diocese, filed articles of incorporation whereby he, as the bishop of Reno, became a religious corporation sole. His successor in that office, Bishop Robert Dwyer, is now that corporation sole, through which all goods of the Reno diocese are held.

The corporation sole act was passed for the express purpose of giving churches in Nevada an easy and safe method of holding their property, wide enough in scope to include all individual ecclesiastical disciplines. The only purpose for which a corporation sole may be formed in Nevada is the "acquiring, holding or disposing of church or religious society property, for the benefit of religion, for works of charity, and for public worship."[37]

The law specifies that the corporation sole shall be vested in the person who holds the office mentioned in the articles of the incorporation. "Upon making and filing for record articles of incorporation as herein provided, the person subscribing the same, and his successor in office by the name or title specified in the articles, shall thereafter be deemed, and is hereby created, a body politic and a corporation sole, with continual perpetual succession."[38] Thus in Nevada, when Bishop Gorman subscribed articles of incorporation as the Roman Catholic Bishop of Reno, the corporation sole was vested in his person. However, Bishop Gorman was the corporation sole only by virtue of his office. Though the corporation was vested in his person, he did not have the type of absolute ownership which a fee simple gives. Accordingly, when Bishop Gorman was transferred to the Diocese of Dallas-Fort Worth, he ceased to be the corporation sole in Nevada, because he ceased to hold the office of Bishop of Reno. This mode of tenure, then, secures the ecclesiastical property in the moral person, the diocese, although it does

for purposes of exemptions charity is said to include religious objects and purposes.

[37] NRS. 84.010.

[38] NRS. 84.040.

not actually vest the dominion of that property in the moral person, but in a physical person. *De iure* the ownership of church property is vested in a physical person, the bishop, but *de facto* this is equivalent to vesting the ownership in a moral person, the diocese, because it is only so long as he is the head of that diocese that the physical person is the corporation sole, holding the property of the diocese.

It is clear that a corporation sole mode of tenure fails to match the provisions of canon law. The Code decrees that all ecclesiastical property shall be owned by a moral ecclesiastical person. Civil law here vests legal title in a physical person. Secondly, canon law envisions a mode of tenure whereby each parish, as a moral person, will own the property of that parish. But in a corporation sole system the bishop is made the administrator of all ecclesiastical goods in the diocese thus incorporated. The Code declares that the bishop is the ordinary administrator only of that property which is strictly diocesan in nature. The pastor is the ordinary administrator of the property of his parish; the bishop has a supervisory capacity through which he is to watch vigilantly over the administration of parish property by the immediate administrators of the property, the pastors.[39]

Nevertheless, a corporation sole system, although it vests the powers of acquisition, tenure, and administration of ecclesiastical goods differently from the provisions of canon law, actually leaves the bishop free to administer such property according to the Code. Thus the bishop has the power, in civil law, to turn the ordinary administration of the property attached to each parish over to its pastor. The civil law looks upon the bishop as the owner and administrator of the property of each parish. This does not prevent the bishop from looking upon the parish as the moral person holding dominion, according to canon law, of such property and the pastor as its ordinary administrator. In this way the provisions of canon law are fulfilled in practice legally within the frame-work of a civil jurisdiction which *de iure* establishes an uncanonical method.

One common objection to corporation sole tenure of church property was the fact that "the power of the English corporation sole to take property was restricted to real property as distinguished

[39] Canon 1519; Cf. *infra*, p. 114.

from personal property."[40] However, such a limitation is not included in the Nevada corporation sole statute. Among the powers of the corporation sole in Nevada is the power "to acquire and possess, by donation, gift, bequest, devise or purchase, and to hold and maintain property, real, personal and mixed, and to grant, sell, convey, rent, or otherwise dispose of the same as may be necessary to carry on or promote the objects of the corporation."[41] This Nevada law, therefore, gives the Church unlimited control over its property. The statute is entirely devoid of any mortmain provisions, and is most praiseworthy in that it extends to the Church, through the bishop who is the corporation sole, the same liberty which the Nevada constitution grants to all natural persons and recognizes as their natural and inalienable right, namely that of "acquiring, possessing and protecting property."[42] The Nevada statute gives the bishop, as the corporation sole, the power "to buy, sell, lease, mortgage, and in every way deal in real and personal property in the same manner that a natural person may, and without the order of any court."[43]

This freedom of administration, granted to the bishop civilly, means that he is free to administer the property according to the dictates of canon law, and indeed, the civil law fully expects that the church property will be administered according to the discipline of the particular Church incorporated under it and extends such wide powers, unencumbered by civil restrictions and formalities, for that very purpose. While the Nevada courts have had no occasion to make a ruling in the matter, it is to be fully expected that these courts would leave all matters of internal Church discipline, including that on matters of administration of church property, up to the decision of the ecclesiastical authority or tribunal which has jurisdiction in the case. The history of the civil decisions in the federal and state courts throughout the country has been to accept and support the decision handed down by the highest authority within the ecclesiastical jurisdiction in all matters of internal discipline. The civil courts will determine property rights of religious bodies and will protect them, but in so far as any controversy is ecclesiastical, even controversies concerning temporalities, the civil courts have

40 Brown, pp. 147-148.

41 NRS. 84.050.

42 *Nevada Constitution,* Art. I, Sect. 1.

43 NRS. 84.050.

steadfastly recognized the jurisdiction of the ecclesiastical court in determining the controversy.[44]

The United States Supreme Court, for example, invoked the decision of the highest Church court as definitive in the case of Watson vs. Jones in 1871. The court stated:

> The rule of action which should govern the civil courts, founded in a broad and sound view of the relations of Church and State under our system of laws and supported by a preponderating weight of judicial authority is that, whenever the question of discipline or of faith or ecclesiastical rule, custom and law has been decided by the highest of these church judicatories to which the matter has been carried, the legal tribunals must accept such decisions as final, and as binding on them, in their application to the case before them.[45]

Again as recently as 1952, the Supreme Court followed a similar line of reasoning in the case of Kedroff vs. St. Nicholas Cathedral, where it declared:

> There are occasions when civil courts must draw lines between the responsibilities of church and state for the disposition or use of property. Even in these cases when the property right follows as an incident from decisions of the church custom or law on ecclesiastical issues, the church rule controls. This under our constitution necessarily follows in order that there may be free exercise of religion.[46]

Another very clear declaration of reference by the civil court to the decision of the ecclesiastical court, when property or civil rights depend upon an interpretation of the ecclesiastical law, occurs in Lamb vs. Cain:

[44] Cf. Elston vs. Wilburn, 208 Ark. 277, 186 S.W. 2d. 662 (1945); Ragsdall vs. Church of Christ in Eldora, 244, Iowa 474, 55 N.W. 2d. 539 (1952); Klix vs. Polish Roman Catholic St. Stanislaus, 137 Mo. App. 247, 188 S.W. 1171 (1909); Lamb vs. Cain, 129 Ind. 486, 28 N.E. 13 (1891); First Presbyterian Church of Lincoln vs. First Cumberland Presbyterian Church of Lincoln, 245 Ill. 74, 91 N.E. 761 (1910); Gonzalez vs. Roman Catholic Archbishop of Manila, 280 U.S. 1, 50 S. Ct. 5, 74 L. Ed. 131 (1929); Watson vs. Jones, 80 U.S. 679, 20 L. Ed. 666 (1871); Jandron vs. Zuendel, 139 Fed. Sup. 887 (1955); Kedroff vs. St. Nicholas Cathedral, 344 U.S. 94, 73 S. Ct. 143, 97 L. Ed. 120 (1952).

[45] Watson vs. Jones, 80 U.S. 679, 20 L. Ed. 666 (1871).

[46] Kedroff vs. St. Nicholas Cathedral, 344, U.S.94, 73 S.Ct.143, 97 L.Ed.120 (1952).

> From these considerations the rule in this country has become elementary that when a civil right depends upon some matter pertaining to ecclesiastical affairs, the civil tribunal tries the right, and nothing more, taking the ecclesiastical decisions out of which the right has arisen as it finds them, and accepts such decisions as matters adjudicated by another legally constituted jurisdiction.[47]

The right of the Church to legislate and follow its own particular rules even in temporal affairs, because of its constitutionally guaranteed freedom, was brought out in the case of Klix vs. Polish Roman Catholic St. Stanislaus. The court said:

> Many religious sects, and among them the Roman Catholic, are of world-wide extent and vast membership, with congregations, parishes, and established hierarchies and councils in every land. For ages they have observed a uniform policy, not only in spiritual matters, but in the transaction of secular business and the management of their properties. To force upon them an unaccustomed economy would introduce confusion and embarrassment; whereas to refuse them corporate capacity, except on the conditions of renouncing their customs would be illiberal treatment by the state . . . A statutory alteration of the form of church government may not constitute interference with matters of faith; yet, nonetheless, the right of every religious sect to preserve the peculiar economy it prefers, and perhaps has obeyed immemorially, touches closely if it is not part of, that religious freedom which American Constitutions guarantee.[48]

Accordingly, it may be argued that the Nevada corporation sole law is meant to be used by the Catholic Church in Nevada within the frame-work of the provisions of the Code of canon law. The bishop is not prevented, then, from observing the law of the Code that the pastor is the ordinary administrator of the property of his parish, even though the Nevada law makes the bishop the administrator of such property. The civil law may be said to presume that the bishop will administer church property according to the regu-

[47] Lamb vs. Cain, 129 Ind. 486, 28 N. E. 13 (1891).

[48] Klix vs. Polish Roman Catholic St. Stanislaus, 137, Mo. App. 347, 118 S.W. 1171 (1909).

lations of the Code, that is, mediately in the instance of parochial goods, rather than immediately.[49]

One point very strongly in favor of corporation sole as a mode of tenure of church property is the fact that it provides for perpetual succession. One of the big difficulties experienced with other methods in American civil law has been the problem of transferring the property to the bishops' successors. This was especially true in places where property was held in fee simple. Corporation sole laws were passed as a sure means of guaranteeing that church property would remain in the hands of churches throughout all hierarchical changes. [50]

The Nevada corporation sole law is very explicit on this point. It states that the person subscribing the articles of incorporation is a body politic and a corporation sole, and that so are his successors in the office named in the articles a corporation sole "with continual perpetual succession."[51] The law provides that, when the person who is the corporation sole dies, resigns, or is removed from the office by reason of which he is the corporation sole (provided that such removal has been made by the person or body having the authority to remove him), "his successor in office, as such corporation sole, shall be vested with the title to any and all property held by his predecessor, as such corporation sole, with like power and authority over the same, and subject to all the legal liabilities and obligations with reference thereto."[52]

The one lacuna regarding perpetuity, which may be said to exist in this statute, is the lack of legislation for the period of the vacancy of the episcopal see. It could be argued that during the vacancy of the see the church property is held by no one, but the title is held in abeyance by the state until such time as the office of bishop is filled. This lacuna, however, presents virtually no problem in Nevada, because the articles by which the Bishop of Reno was incorporated designate that during such vacancy the diocesan administrator, named according to the regulations of canon law, "shall function and act as the incumbent of the Corporation Sole."[53] While

[49] For a more detailed treatment of the attitude of the civil courts toward ecclesiastical discipline and rights read McGrath, "Canon Law and American Church Law: A Comparative Study," *The Jurist,* XVIII (1958), 260-270.

[50] Cf. *supra,* p. 92.

[51] NRS. 84.040.

[52] NRS. 84.080.

[53] Cf. *supra,* p. 92.

it cannot be argued from this provision in the articles of incorporation that the diocesan administrator holds the legal title, as such, to the church property, he is empowered to administer that property just as if he did hold such legal title, and no restrictions on his power of administration are mentioned in the articles. In practice, then, he would be able to carry on the administration of the church property just as fully as the bishop can, subject, however, to the limitations placed on him by canon law. Thus the perpetuity of church property has the full protection of Nevada civil law and all danger of its falling out of ecclesiastical control is removed.

This provision may be considered defective in so far as it fails to provide for the period before the administrator is elected. The diocesan consultors, to whom the regimen passes, should not be constrained by the articles of incorporation to elect an administrator before the time allotted to them by the code (eight days) is up.

They might well prefer to perform some act of administration themselves rather than leave it to the administrator. Obviously, some matter might have to be decided during the eight-day period, a note come due or the like, and the law should not force the consultors to elect an administrator before that period is completed in order to perform such necessary acts of administration. Furthermore, one must inquire into what provision is made here for the vicar general *sede plena* or *sede impedita*. It might be argued that, in so far as canon law gives him power to act for the bishop, the civil law would uphold his acts of administration, allowing the church rule to control. But is seems that such situations should be more explicitly covered in the articles of incorporation or in the wording of the law itself, perhaps by referring to the ordinary or to the possessor of ordinary power and thereby including the vicar general.

In general, however, it may be said that, although the Church in Nevada is incorporated under a method given only secondary approval by the Holy See, the rights of the Church in property matters seem to be well safeguarded. The Church authorities are in actual fact able to acquire, hold, and especially administer the temporalities of the Church quite closely within the frame-work of canon law.

Section III. Application of Religious Corporation Act of 1867

The other corporation act in Nevada law available to churches for incorporations is the act of 1867, entitled "An Act to provide for the incorporation of religious, charitable, literary, scientific, and other associations."[54] Section I of this act states:

> It shall be lawful for all churches, congregations, religious, moral, beneficial, charitable, literary, or scientific associations or societies, by such rules and methods as their rules, regulations, or discipline may direct, to appoint or elect any number, not less than three nor more than fifteen, as trustees or directors, to take charge of the estate and property belonging thereto, and to transact all affairs relative to the temporalities thereof.[55]

It is clear from this statute that a church incorporated under this act would be a corporation aggregate. Accordingly, more thorough examination of the provision of this law is necessary in order to determine if perchance its regulations make it similar to the *Parish Corporation,* as devised in New York. If this law is similar to the New York law, then the churches in Nevada should be incorporated under it according to the 1911 directive of the Sacred Congregation of the Council.[56]

The New York law explicitly names that the archbishop or bishop, the vicar general, the rector of the parish, and two laymen from the parish selected by the first three should execute and acknowledge the certificate of incorporation of the church, and also specifies that these same five persons are to be the trustees of the corporation. The Nevada law is not so specific in this matter, but such a course is certainly legal within its provisions. The Nevada law merely says that there must be at least three trustees and no more than fifteen. It leaves the manner of their appointment or election up to the particular rules of the church incorporating. Thus, for example, under this act the Catholic Church could determine that the bishop, his vicar general, and the pastor or administrator of the incorporating parish shall be trustees by virtue of their office, and that two laymen, members of the parish, shall be selected to be additional trustees, bringing the total number of trustees to five. The manner of selection of the two lay trustees could be accomplished by the vote of a majority of such officials. They could also be selected by the bis-

[54] Bonnified and Healey, *The Compiled Laws of the State of Nevada* (1873), p. 447.

[55] NRS. 86.100.

[56] *Digest,* II, 444-445.

hop after hearing the opinion of the vicar general and the pastor, a method which, it seems, would be more in harmony with canon law.

Thus far this Nevada law, then conforms to the New York law. The parish itself, for example, Roman Catholic Church of St. Albert the Great (Reno, Nevada), would be incorporated with all the members considered as incorporators. Administrative powers for the management of the temporal affairs of the church would be vested in the trustees, as they are in the New York system. Furthermore, it could be explicitly mentioned in the articles of incorporation that the lay trustees are to be elected annually, and that the successors to the offices of the bishop, vicar general, and pastor of said parish, shall by the very fact of their succession be trustees of the corporation.

The Nevada law also provides for the perpetual succession of all the church property, declaring that "All lands, tenements, and hereditaments that have been or may hereafter be, lawfully conveyed . . . to any persons or trustees in trust for use of any such organization, shall descend, with the improvements, in perpetual succession to, and shall be held by such trustees in trust for such organization."[57] Although the Nevada law contains no specific provision for administration during the vacancy of the episcopal see as the New York Statute does, there is nothing in the law to prevent such regulations being included in the articles of incorporation. Similarly, the rule could be included in the articles that no act or proceeding of the trustees of the incorporated church shall be valid without the sanction of the bishop of the diocese, or in the case of his absence or inability to act, without the sanction of the vicar general or the administrator of the diocese.[58] This rule is expressed in the New York statute. It would be a lawful rule under the Nevada law, if it were included in the articles of incorporation, or in the bylaws of the trustees, or the synodal legislation of the diocese.

The powers of the trustees in the Nevada law are as broad as the powers granted trustees in the New York law, and in one respect even broader. The New York law demands that the religious corporation is not to sell or mortgage or lease for a term of five years any of its real property without first obtaining the permission of the Supreme Court.[59] The Nevada law allows the trustees to lease

[57] NRS. 86.150.

[58] *N.Y. Religious Corporations Law*, #91.

[59] *N.Y. Religious Corporations Law*, #12, sub. 1.

real property without any court order; but it does require the permission of the district court, in which the incorporated church is located, before selling or mortgaging any real estate of the church.[60] This requirement of a court order for the sale or mortgaging of church property dates back to Queen Elizabeth, when laws were passed restraining the power of churches to alienate their property and is considered to have been brought to New York by the colonists.[61] This enactment impairs a common law right of the corporation, and for that reason has been interpreted strictly by New York courts. It may be presumed that Nevada courts would look to the New York interpretations for precedent (the law has not been judicially tested in Nevada), since apparently New York is the only other State in which the law is found.[62]

Except for this limitation of their freedom of administration, the trustees are granted broad powers by the Nevada law. Among these powers is included the right to take into their possession and custody all the temporalities of the corporation, to sue and be sued, to receive and hold all churches, burying places, halls, school houses, hospitals, or other buildings, as well as all estates and appurtenances belonging to the parish. They can lease real estate, improve the property, erect any building necessary to carry out the objects of the parish, have a common seal and alter it at pleasure, and perform all the duties imposed upon them by the regulation of the Church.[63]

These powers make no specific mention of the rights of the bishop to divide parishes, creating new parishes from the area formerly assigned the old parish, and to divide the property and income equitably between the old and new parish. The general provision granting the trustees power to perform all duties imposed upon them by the rules of the Church could be said to include such a specific power as this; however, it would be safer to mention this power explicitly in the articles of incorporation. The New York law declares

[60] NRS. 86.130.

[61] Murphy, p. 76; Zollman, "Powers of American Religious Corporations," *Michigan Law Review*, XIII (1915), 657.

[62] Interpretations of the New York courts may be seen in Murphy, pp. 76-78. Since many early Nevada legislators were New Yorkers, it is probable that the enactment was taken from the New York law. Consider that the New York law was passed in 1863, just four years before the Nevada law, although this type of limitation of religious corporations had been practiced in New York from the Colony days. Furthermore, the limitation on leases running more than five years was added to the New York statute only in 1953, and this provision is missing from the Nevada statute.

[63] NRS. 86.120.

that the bishop has this power of division of parishes, independently of any action or consent on the part of the trustees of the original parish, a provision which is consonant with canon law.[64]

It is clear that this Nevada law has a great deal of similarity to the New York law. It lacks the specific mention of many provisions of the New York legislation, but it places no legal obstacle to their inclusion in the articles of incorporation. However, the Nevada law does contain two other regulations, which are not found in the New York law and which make it an undesirable vehicle for the incorporation of Catholic churches in Nevada.

The first of these provisions is a mortmain law, which limits the amount of property which a church incorporated under this act can hold. Section 7 of the act reads:

> The real estate held by such association or corporation shall in no case exceed one block in any town or city, and ten acres in the country; nor shall any portion thereof used for ordinary business purposes, and connected with the objects of such association or corporations, or rented for profit, be exempted from taxation; provided:
>
> 1. That the grand lodges of the orders of Free and Accepted Masons and of the Independent Order of Odd Fellows, and subordinate lodges thereof, may acquire and hold such real and personal property as may be deemed necessary for the proper authorities thereof to carry out their charitable, educational or ceremonial objects; and such association or corporation may sue and be sued, and have such other general powers as are by the laws of this state granted to corporations.
>
> 2. That all real personal property owned by such association or corporation prior to March 2, 1867, notwithstanding any of the provisions of NRS. 86.100 to 86.170, inclusive, may be still held, owned and enjoyed by them.[65]

The second of these provisions imposes the duty on the trustees to make an annual report of all real and personal property held in trust by them and of the condition of the corporation to the society or association. They must file a copy of this report in the county

[64] *N.Y. Religious Corporations Law,* #92; canon 1427.

[65] NRS. 86.100.

clerk's office, with an affidavit of the truth of such report and also a statement that the corporation has not been engaged, directly or indirectly, in any other business than such as is set forth in the original certificate on file in the county clerk's office.[66]

The mortmain law, limiting the amount of property which the corporation can hold to one block in a city or town and ten acres in the country, is clearly discriminatory. It infringes on the Church's right to acquire and hold property. The fact that the very law contains a special exception from this restriction for one group is evidence of the very bad faith in which the law was conceived. This statute is not worthy of a state which is justly proud of the freedoms it grants and safeguards for all groups without discrimination.

It is quite clear that it would be impossible for the Catholic Church to seek to incorporate its various parishes, and the diocese itself as well, under this act, as long as this unjust restrictive provision remained a part of it. Some parishes in Nevada currently own larger tracts of land than are allowed by this statute; strictly diocesan property far outreaches it. Indeed, it is hard to conceive how a law can in one place say that a corporation has the power to possess churches, burying places, halls, school houses, hospitals and other buildings, and in another place legislate that it must somehow manage to situate all this property within one city block. It should be promptly removed from the Nevada law books.

The second provision places a burden on the trustees, which is really a matter of the private discipline of the Church. The church holdings are not a public trust, but a private one. The regulations of canon law call for similar reports to be made by the parishes to the bishop.[67] It is at best a needless repetition to ask that the bishop and other trustees make copies of these reports, make affidavits to their truth, and sign statements that the parishes and diocese have been carrying on works of religion and charity exclusively. Does it not also imply a certain lack of confidence on the part of the State in the integrity of Nevada's churches?

The Diocese of Reno, therefore could not incorporate under this act as it now stands.[68] However, if the two aforementioned provisions were removed from the law, it would merit serious considera-

[66] NRS. 86.170.

[67] Canon 1522.

[68] The Sisters of Our Lady of Mount Carmel in Reno have incorporated under

tion as providing a mode of tenure declared more perferable by the Sacred Congregation of 1911.

There is one other possibility which could be examined for the incorporation of Catholic churches in Nevada. This is the fact that Nevada legislatures have passed thirteen acts for the incorporation of specific churches, fraternal orders, and other organizations. Among these are the Protestant Episcopal Church, the Free and Accepted Masons, the Independent Order of Odd Fellows, Knights of Pythias, American Legion, Boy Scouts of America, Veterans of Foreign Wars and others.[69] Particular rules, adapted to the special needs of these organizations, were passed by the legislatures regarding their incorporation, their methods of acquiring, holding, and administering their temporalities. With precedent such as this in Nevada legislation, there is ample justification, and every hope of success, for presenting to the legislature for passage a special act for the incorporation of Roman Catholic Dioceses and Churches in Nevada. Such an act would contain the provisions of canon law in explicit terms, and thus bring about a truer concordance between civil and canon law in matters relating to church property.

Another recommendation might be to incorprate each parish separately as a corporation sole, as the Pastor of Immaculate Conception Parish, a Corporation Sole. There is nothing in Nevada law to prevent such individual corporation. Such a system at first glance may seem to conform more with canon law than simply incorporating the whole diocese as a corporation sole. In basic set-up, at least, it does approach the *Parish Corporation* plan more closely than does the present diocesan corporation sole. However, in effect, this system is farther from the desires of the Code. To incorporate each pastor as a corporation sole would be to remove all control over the pastor's administration from the bishop. In civil law the bishop would be unable to enforce his powers of vigilance over the administration of the pastor. The bishop would still have canonical control over the pastors, but in a case of maladministration, he would have no civil means to regain property or funds which the pastor had disposed of in some manner harmful to the welfare of the Church or the parish. To remove all control from the hands of the ordinary is far from the method of tenure desired by the Code. The

this act. They are the only Catholic Institution in Nevada to have utilized it.

[69] Cf. *supra*, pp. 46-47.

establishment of a great number of parish corporations sole in the diocese may seem on paper to come closer to the *Parish Corporation* plan given first preferance by the Sacred Congregation, but in practice it would be found to be much farther removed from that system of tenure than is the present diocesan corporation sole system.

CHAPTER V

ADMINISTRATION OF CHURCH PROPERTY

ARTICLE I. CANON LAW ON ADMINISTRATION

Church property is always held by an ecclesiastical moral person.[1] These moral persons have the status of minors.[2]The ownership of church property, then, is vested in minors. In Church law, as in civil law, the property of minors is not administered by the minors themselves, but by their legally appointed guardians or administrators. Thus, trustees, directors or administrators are named to care for the goods of all moral legal persons.

Accordingly, the ownership of church property "in effect approaches trusteeship."[3] The moral person, who owns the church goods, cannot use and dispose such goods freely, as a private person can. These goods were acquired for a specific purpose, for works of religion or charity, and their use and disposition is regulated by their special purposes. Canon law, therefore, names administrators to govern the use and disposition of church property. These administrators "act in the manner of trustees who exercise authority over church property by devoting it to the purposes for which the Church acquired it. In this sense they hold it in trust. The Supreme Court of Ohio in the case, Mannix vs. Purcell, alluded to this trust relationship when it accepted the canons and decrees of the Church as evidence that a trust existed. The Court stated that 'the parties have gone back fifteen centuries into the laws of canons of the Church for proof of the nature of the tenure by which the Archbishop held the legal title to ecclesiastical property; and the proof is overwhelming that he was not invested with an absolute title to it as his own. It is practically conceded that he held it in trust . . .' "[4]

In this article we will treat the regulations of the Code concerning administrators and various contracts through which church property is administered.

1 Canon 1499,§2.

2 Canon 100,§3.

3 Woywod, II, 202.

4 Wiggins, *Property Laws of the State of Ohio Affecting the Church,* The Catholic University of America Canon Law Studies, n. 367 (Washington, D.C.: The Catholic University of America Press, 1956), p. 97 (hereafter cited Wiggins); Mannix vs. Purcell, 46 Ohio State 102.

Section I. Administrators

A. The Roman Pontiff

The Roman Pontiff is the supreme administrator and dispenser of all ecclesiastical goods.[5] The pope is not the owner of all church property, but because of his primacy of jurisdiction he does have the right of administration over it. He administers the property which belongs to the Universal Church and to the Apostolic See through the Roman Curia. He administers other church property through the various administrators of the individual moral persons in the Church, whose acts of administration he controls through the general regulations for administration laid down in the Code, and by keeping a close watch over their execution. He also reserves some more important administrative acts to himself, for example, the alienation of goods valued at more than five thousand dollars.[6] The function of administration entails the preservation and improvement of the property, the natural or artificial production of fruits or income from it, and the useful application of such fruits or income to the proper persons.[7]

B. The Local Ordinary

The local ordinary has the duty of diligently supervising the administration of all ecclesiastical goods in his territory, except those things which have been withdrawn from his jurisdiction. Legitimate prescription granting him greater rights has full force. Within the limits of the common law and with due regard for the acquired rights of others, legitimate customs and circumstances, he shall issue appropriate instructions for the regulation of all matters pertaining to the administration of the church property in his territory.[8]

The local ordinary is not described by the Code as the administrator of the church property in his diocese, as the pope is described as the administrator of all the goods of the Church. The Code rather speaks of the local ordinary in terms of a supervisor or inspector. His is the duty of vigilance, which includes making regulations for administration. The right and obligation of ordinary administration is vested in the person who holds the office to which that duty is attached, as the pastor of a parish. The local ordinary is the immedi-

[5] Canon 1518.

[6] Canon 1532.

[7] Bouscaren, p. 822.

[8] Canon 1519.

ate administrator of all the property which constitutes the episcopal benefice, of all funds held in common for the benefit of the diocese, all funds belonging to the diocesan seminary, and with his consultors of the property of his cathedral church.[9]

C. Diocesan Council of Administration

To assist him in the proper discharge of this supervisory office, the ordinary shall provide for a council of administration. Members of this board shall include the ordinary himself, who will be its president, and two or more capable men, who, as far as possible should be skilled in both canon and civil law. The ordinary shall select the members of the board after consultation with his diocesan consultors, unless some equivalent provision for their appointment has been established by particular law or custom. Persons related to the ordinary in the first or second degree of consanguinity of affinity may not be appointed to this council, except by an Apostolic indult. When any more important administrative act is to be performed, the ordinary shall not fail to consult the council of administration. The vote of these members of the board, however, is merely consultative, unless their consent is expressly required by the common law or in the charter of a foundation. The members of this council must take an oath in the presence of the ordinary that they will fulfill their office efficiently and faithfully.[10]

In many dioceses in the United States the diocesan consultors are also the council of administration. However, laymen may be named to the board. The advice or consent, depending on the importance or value of the property involved, of the council of administration is required of the ordinary in the erection of benefices, the alienation of goods, the sale or exchange of sacred objects, the leasing of some ecclesiastical goods, and before making an appearance in court in the name of the cathedral church or the *mensa episcopalis.*[11] It is, of course, most practical and useful to consult men experienced in the business of real estate and the regulations of civil law before acting in matters of church property. Even when laymen, who are expert in these matters, are not *ex officio* members of the council of administration, it is the wise practice of most ordinaries

[9] Cf. canons 1472 ff.; 1375; 1359; 427; 1182,§1; Bouscaren, p. 823; Woywod, II, 202-203. For the rule governing the administration of property owned by religious, see canons 531-537.

[10] Canon 1520.

[11] Cf. canons 1415,§2; 1532; 1539,§2; 1541,§2; 1653,§1.

to hear their advice before taking final action in such matters, where mistakes can be very costly and harmful to all the members of the diocese.

D. Local Board of Administration

Besides the diocesan council of administration, the local ordinary must also appoint some prudent and qualified men of good reputation for the administration of the property of any church or pious institute for which no administrator is provided by law or by the charter of foundation. They should be changed after three years, unless local circumstances direct a longer or shorter term of office. However, if laymen participate in the administration of ecclesiastical property, either by lawful title of foundation or by the free appointment of the local ordinary, the administration shall nevertheless be entirely transacted in the name of the Church, and the ordinary has the right of visitation, of demanding an account, and of prescribing the manner of administration.[12]

Before they assume their duties, these local administrators must take an oath in the presence of the ordinary or the vicar forane that they will perform their work of administration faithfully and efficiently. They must also prepare an accurate and itemized inventory of all immovable property, all precious movable goods, and all other property, with a description and evaluation of each; this inventory must be signed by all the administrators. They may use an old inventory, but in this case they must check it carefully and indicate all things which have been lost and all new things which have been acquired. One copy of this inventory must be kept in the archives of the diocesan curia and another copy in the archives of the administration.[13]

These special local administrators are appointed in the situation when a church or pious institute has no ordinary administrator by law or by the charter of foundation. The pastor is the ordinary administrator of his parish, as is the rector or head of a pious institution.[14] The ordinary is free to remove the administrators before their three-year term of office is completed or to extend the term, if circumstances should make either action advisable. A local board of

[12] Canon 1521.

[13] Canon 1522.

[14] Cf. canons 1182, 1476, 1489.

administration could not be composed entirely of laymen, but it is probable that one cleric on the board is sufficient.[15]

In the United States pastors sometimes are assisted in the administration of the parish by two or more lay trustees. According to the norms of the Third Council of Baltimore,[16] all matters concerning these lay trustees, their manner of appointment, number, term of office, is to be regulated by the statutes of each individual diocese. Diocesan institutions for charity and welfare usually have a much larger board of directors.[17] Such lay trustees should not be confused with the local board of Administrators. The former assist an administrator; the latter are appointed to administrate in the absence of an ordinary administrator.

E. Duties of Administrators

Administrators are bound to fulfill their office with the care and diligence of a good father of a family. Hence they must:

(1) guard against any loss of the church property entrusted to their care or against any damage to it;

(2) observe the rules of canon and civil law, as well as all provisions made by a founder or donor or legitimate authority;

(3) collect the fruits and income of the goods diligently and at the proper times, keep them in a safe place, and use them according to the intention of the founder or according to existing laws and regulations;

(4) invest the surplus revenue of a church (moral person), with the consent of the ordinary, to the benefit of the church;

(5) keep well-ordered books of all receipts and expenditures;

(6) keep the documents and legal papers upon which the property rights of the moral person rest in the archives or in a suitable and proper safe; where it can be readily done, authentic copies of all such papers should also be kept in the archives or safe of the curia[18]

[15] Abbo-Hannan, II, 726; Coronata, *Institutiones Iuris Canonici* (5 vols., Vol. I, 4.ed., 1950, Vol. II, 4.ed., 1951, Romae: Marietti), II, no. 1062, p. 475 (hereafter cited Coronata).

[16] *Acta et Decreta Concilii Baltimorensis Textii, A.D. MDCCCLXXXIV* (Baltimorae: Typis Joannis Murphy et Sociorum, 1886), n. 287.

[17] Woywod, II, 204. Cf. canons 1182-1184.

[18] Canon 1523.

As all are bound to pay employees a just wage, this obligation falls with special emphasis on all clerics, religious, and administrators of church property. The Church is expected to set an example of social justice. Accordingly, administrators must pay an adequate, just wage to their workingmen, give them sufficient free time to perform their religious duties at a convenient hour; they shall make no arrangements which interfere with the workers' family duties or their efforts to save money; they shall not impose on them any burdens which are beyond their physical capacity or not suited to their age or sex.[19]

All administrators, both clerics and laymen, are bound to make an annual report of their administration to the local ordinary. No custom contrary to this provision may excuse its neglect. This includes the administration of any church, including the cathedral church, of any canonically erected pious place, or of a confraternity. If under particular law an accounting must also be made to others specifically designated, then the local ordinary must be included among these, and any release from this obligation is of absolutely no juridical value to the administrators.[20]

Churches and church property which belong to exempt religious would not be included in the demands of this canon; however, property which is owned by a parish and merely attended by exempt religious would be included in the regulation.[21] Particular law which could demand such a report made to other designated persons could be the charter of a foundation or a statute of civil law.[22]

Administrators may not begin a lawsuit in the name of the church, nor act as defenders in one, without first obtaining the written permission of the local ordinary; however, in an urgent case, they may obtain the permission of the vicar forane, who must then inform the ordinary immediately of the permission granted.[23] This prohibition includes lawsuits in ecclesiastical courts, as well as civil suits.[24] Although the defense of the rights of the church is part of ordinary

[19] Canon 1524.

[20] Canon 1525.

[21] Cf. canons 533,§1; 535,§3; 615; 630,§3 and 4; 1425.

[22] Cf. *supra*, pp. 107-108.

[23] Canon 1526.

[24] Abbo-Hannan, II, 730.

administration, the permission is required because of the great importance and far-reaching effects of such suits.[25]

Administrators act invalidly, whenever they exceed the limits and methods of ordinary administration, unless they have previously obtained the written permission of the ordinary. The Church is not liable for contracts made by administrators without the permission of the competent superior, except when and in so far as the Church has profited from them.[26]

Ordinary administration includes what is necessary for the preservation of the church property, all contracts and payments for their regular maintenance, the collection of debts, rents, interest, or dividends which regularly accrue from such property, payment of current bills and taxes. "Ordinary acts of administration also include such acts as are to be done at fixed intervals (monthly, quarterly, annually) as well as those which are necessary for the customary transaction of business."[27]

Extraordinary administration would include acts of alienation, the acceptance or refusal of a gift or bequest, construction of new buildings or extensive repairs on old buildings, opening a cemetery, investment of capital, opening a school or hopsital or other parochial institution, taking up special collections.[28] Also, synodal legislation in the diocese could name certain acts, as extraordinary, needing the ordinary's permission, such as spending a sum of money in excess of five hundred dollars.[29]

Even though they are not obliged by reason of an ecclesiastical benefice or office, administrators who have expressly or tacitly accepted their office and then relinquish it of their own accord with resulting harm to the Church must make restitution.[30]

Section II. Contracts Regarding Church Property

The regulations of civil law concerning general or specific contracts, both named and unnamed, and concerning payments, shall be

[25] Bouscaren, p. 827.

[26] Canon 1527.

[27] Bouscaren, p. 828; Cf. also Abbo-Hannan, II, 731; Vromant, *De Bonis Ecclesiae Temporalibus* (3.ed., Burges-Paris: Desclee de Brouwer, 1953, p. 185 (hereafter cited Vromant).

[28] Abbo-Hannan, II, 731.

[29] Bouscaren, p. 829. Cf. *Diocese of Reno First Synod* (Reno, Nevada: 1858), nn.140-141.

[30] Canon 1528.

observed in ecclesiastical matters as if enacted by canon law and with the same effects, except those regulations which are contrary to the divine law or unless canon law has decreed otherwise.[31] Thus, whatever the civil law determines to be necessary for the validity or liceity of a contract is also required in canon law. The various civil statutes concerning the capacity of persons to contract, the proper matter for contracts, required consent and formalities, exchange of a valuable consideration, lawful consideration and object, manner of fulfilling an obligation assumed, etc., are all canonized by the Code; they have the same canonical force as if they were canons in the Code. Civil statutes concerning contracts, however, which are contrary to divine law, such as the sale of stolen goods, are not canonized. Also excepted are any civil statutes concerning contracts, which are contrary to some regulation of canon law. Thus canonical requirements for alienation of church property must be observed regardless of any civil rule on the matter. In practically all cases both the civil and canonical requirements can easily be met in this matter.[32]

A. Alienation

Safeguarding the ruling of canon 1281,§1, which requires the permission of the Apostolic See for the valid alienation or transfer of important relics and precious images, the following conditions are required for the alienation of movable and immovable church property which is imperishable:

(1) a written appraisal of the property must be made by reliable experts;

(2) a just reason for the alienation, that is, urgent necessity, evident advantage of the Church, piety;

(3) the permission of the legitimate superior, without which the alienation is invalid.

Also, all other opportune precautions, which the superior, as circumstances dictate, should find needful to prevent all loss to the Church, should not be omitted.[33]

[31] Canon 1529.

[32] Bouscaren, p. 830; Abbo-Hannan, II, 733-735, where it is noted that American civil law makes no distinction between named and unnamed contracts, but does recognize implied and quasi-contracts. Abbo-Hannan also list a number of formalities required in most of the American civil jurisdictions.

[33] Canon 1530.

Alienation is used here in its wide meaning, that is, "any lawful act whereby the ownership of church property is transferred to another, or is exposed to the danger of loss, or is withdrawn from the direct possession of the Church for a considerable length of time, or in general, any contract by which church property is placed in a less favorable condition by reason of burdens or obligations imposed upon it."[34]

Alienation includes the following: gifts, sales, exchanges, by which the ownership of property is transferred to another; securities, mortgages, options, compromises, settlements, and other acts which are preparations for alienation; rentals, leases, and acts by which the use of property is transferred; granting the use, usufruct, and various kinds of easements through which property is subjected to burdens *in perpetuum* or for a long time.[35]

However, spending money which is free capital, i.e., not yet invested, to pay debts or make purchases, loaning money at a moderate rate of interest, selling old furniture or vestments, etc., in order to buy new, assuming a mortgage which already burdens newly purchased property, spending money for the purpose for which the donors gave it, refusing to accept a gain or gift—these would not be acts of alienation.[36]

At least two experts must give an appraisal before the alienation of church property, since the canon uses the plural in making this condition. Their appraisals must be in writing, but no oath or other formality is required from them.[37] The legitimate superior, whose permission is required for the validity of the alienation, is the Holy See or local ordinary, as canon 1532 points out.[38]

Church property may not be alienated for a price lower than that specified in the appraisal made by the experts. The alienation should be made by public auction, or at least it should be advertised, unless peculiar circumstances make a different course advisable. The property should be awarded him who, all things considered, made the highest offer. The money received from an alienation is to be

[34] Bouscaren, p. 831.

[35] *Loc. cit.*

[36] *Ibid., pp.* 831-832.

[37] Abbo-Hannan, II, 736; Vermeersch-Creusen, II, no. 835.

[38] Cf. *infra,* p. 120.

invested carefully, safely, and advantageously, for the benefits of the Church.[39]

Sale of church property by auction is not often done in the United States. In some instances, it can be more advantageous to the Church to sell its property secretly, rather than at public auction or after advertising a sale. When such circumstances are present, it is both valid and licit to alienate the property secretly.[40]

The legitimate superior required by canon 1530 for a valid alienation is the Apostolic See when the property involved is a precious object or goods worth more than 30,000 lire or francs.[41] A precious object will be worth at least one thousand francs or in American currency $167.[42] Thirty thousand lire or francs is taken according to the gold value and is figured in this country to mean $6,000 in gold. However, the Sacred Consistorial Congregation, on October 18, 1952, reduced the rate, making it equivalent to five thousand United States dollars at today's evaluation.[43]

When the property to be alienated does not exceed 1,000 lire or francs, the local ordinary may give the necessary permission. However, he must first consult the diocesan board of administration, unless the matter is of little importance, and must also obtain the consent of the interested parties.[44] According to the 1952 notification of the Sacred Consistorial Congregation, one thousand lire or francs may be taken in this country to mean $167 in our currency.[45] A matter of little importance may be taken as something involving fifty dollars or less.[46]

When the property to be alienated is worth more than 1,000 and less than 30,000 lire or francs, that is, when it is valued at between $167 and $5000 in the United States, the local ordinary is the legitimate superior who may give the permission which is required for the validity of the alienation. In this case, the ordinary must first obtain the consent of his diocesan consultors, the diocesan board

39 Canon 1531.

40 Abbo-Hannan, II, 834; Vermeersch-Creusen, II. no. 835; Coronata, II, no. 1071.

41 Canon 1532,§1.

42 S.C. Conc., resol. July 13,1919—*AAS,* XI (1919), 416; *Digest* I, 728-729; Cf. Abbo-Hannan, II, 708; *supra,* p. 49.

43 *Digest.* IV, 391; Bouscaren, 835; Wiggins, p. 111.

44 Canon 1532,§2.

45 *Digest,* IV, 392.

46 Bouscaren, p. 837.

of administration and the interested parties.[47] In the case of the division of divisible goods, the request for permission or consent must state what portions of the goods were already alienated; otherwise the permission is invalid.[48] Furthermore, these formalities, required in canons 1530-1532, are to be fulfilled not only when there is question of the alienation of church property in the strict sense, but also when there is question of entering into any contract by which the Church, or some moral person in the Church, may be placed in a less favorable condition, as in the case of a long-term debt.[49]

The Church has the right to institute a personal action against anyone who has alienated church property without observing the required formalities, and against his heirs as well. If the alienation was invalid, the Church has the right to institute a real action against any possessor of the property; however, the purchaser has the right to claim damages from the administrator who transferred the property to him illegally. The invalid alienation of church property may be contested by the person who transferred it, by his superior, by the successors of either in office, and by any cleric assigned to the church or other ecclesiastical moral person which suffered the loss.[50] Formalities required for licit alienation are evaluation by at least two experts, sale to the highest bidder for a price no lower than that determined by the experts, and a just cause. The proper permission is the only formality required for a valid alienation.

B. Gifts

Prelates and rectors shall not presume to make donations from the movable goods of their churches, except for small and moderate gifts sanctioned by customs, unless there is a just reason, such as remuneration or reward, piety, or Christian charity; otherwise the donations can be revoked by their successors.[51] The giving away of immovable property has already been forbidden, except under specific conditions, by the preceding canons treating alienation. The principle involved here is that the prelates and rectors are administrators, not owners, of church goods. Local custom, or an obligation to benefactors, superiors, or one of charity to the poor or sick especially in times of disaster, are all exceptions to the rule.

47 Canon 1532,§3.
48 Canon 1532,§4.
49 Canon 1533.
50 Canon 1534.
51 Canon 1535.

Unless the contrary is proved, it is to be presumed that donations made to rectors of churches, including those of religious, are made to the church. A donation made to the church cannot be refused by its rector or superior without the permission of the ordinary. If a donation is unlawfully refused, there is legal basis for a suit for restitution *in integrum* or indemnity for any losses suffered on account of the refusal. A donation made to a church and lawfully accepted cannot be recalled because of ingratitude on the part of the prelate or rector.[52]

C. Sale and Exchange

In the sale or exchange of sacred objects no consideration is to be given their consecration or blessing in determining the price. Administrators may exchange negotiable securities payable to bearer for other securities which are safer and more productive or at least equally so, provided that all appearance of bartering and profit-seeking has been excluded. However, the consent of the ordinary, the diocesan board of administration, and the interested parties is required.[53] The sale and exchange of sacred objects, besides being controlled by the general rules for alienation, must not be influenced by the consecration or blessing which these objects may have. Such action would, of course, be simoniacal.[54] Indulgenced articles lose their indulgences when sold, even if no consideration is given the indulegence in determining the price.[55] This canon gives administrators the right to exchange negotiable securities payable to bearer as stocks and bonds, removing such transactions from the general rules for alienation. The administrators must avoid all appearance of carrying on a business, however, and must obtain the required permissions. Canon 142 also requires that they avoid speculation.

Without the special permission of the local ordinary the immovable goods of a church shall not be sold or leased to its administrator or persons related to him in the first or second degree of consanguinity or affinity.[56] The local ordinary's special permission for such sales or leases is required here in order to prevent any possible abuses or scandals arising in the administration of immovable church

[52] Canon 1536.

[53] Canon 1539.

[54] Canon 727,§1.

[55] Canon 924,§2.

[56] Canon 1540.

property. Such a sale or lease, however, without this permission would not be an invalid transaction, but illicit.

D. Leases, Loans, Mortgages, Debts

Sacred objects shall not be loaned for purposes repugnant to their nature.[57] Lending sacred things is not forbidden, so long as the borrower intends to use the sacred objects for a purpose which conforms with their nature.

If, for a legitimate reason, church property is to be pledged or mortgaged, or a debt must be contracted, that legitimate superior whose permission is required by canon 1532[58] must demand that all interested parties be heard first and must also see to it that the debts are paid off as soon as possible. For this purpose the ordinary shall determine the annual rate at which the debt is to be liquidated.[59] Real estate belonging to a church should not be leased except by public auction or after public advertisement, unless special circumstances make a different course advisable.[60] Also, the contract should clearly indicate the exact boundaries of the property to be leased, should specify the nature of the cultivation or care expected, should define the time and method of payment of the rent, and should secure guarantees for the fulfillment of these conditions.[61]

In all leases it is forbidden to collect the rent in advance for more than six months without the permission of the local ordinary. The latter may grant this permission in extraordinary cases, provided he makes prudent regulations, so that such long-term leasing will not cause harm or loss to the church or institution involved or to the successors to the benefice.[62]

In addition, the following regulations must be observed in all leases of church property:

(1) If the value of the lease exceeds 30,000 lire or francs (or $5,000 in the United States) and the term of the lease is more than nine years, the permission of the Apostolic See must be obtained.

(2) If the value of the lease exceeds 30,000 lire or francs ($5,000) but the term of the lease does not exceed nine years, the

[57] Canon 1537.

[58] The Apostolic See or local ordinary; Cf. *supra*, pp. 117, 118, 120.

[59] Canon 1538.

[60] Cf. Canon 1531; *supra*, pp. 119-120.

[61] Canon 1541,§1.

[62] Canon 1479.

local ordinary may grant the permission, but only after obtaining the consent of the diocesan consultors, the diocesan board of administration, and the interested parties.

(3) If the value of the lease is between 1,000 and 30,000 lire or francs ($167 and $5,000 in the United States) and the term of the lease is more than nine years, the local ordinary may grant the permission with the consent of the diocesan consultors, the diocesan board of administration, and the interested parties.

(4) If the value of the lease is between 1,000 and 30,000 lire or francs ($167 and $5,000) and the term of the lease does not exceed nine years, the local ordinary may grant permission after consulting the diocesan board of administration and obtaining the consent of the interested parties.

(5) If the value of the lease does not exceed 1,000 lire or francs ($167) and the term of the lease is more than nine years, the local ordinary may grant the permission after consulting the diocesan board of administration and obtaining the consent of the interested parties.

(6) If the value of the lease does not exceed 1,000 lire or francs ($167) and the term of the lease does not exceed nine years, the lawful administrator may grant the lease after notifying the ordinary.[63]

When a fungible thing is given to another in such a way that it becomes his own and is later to be returned in kind only, no profit may be realized by reason of the contract itself. However, in such a loan it is not *per se* illicit to make an agreement about the legal interest (unless it is evident that the legal rate is exorbitant), nor is it illegal to make an agreement for an even higher rate, provided that there is just and proportionate reason for such an agreement.[64]

Bouscaren comments about this regulation:

> While upholding the traditional teaching of the Church that in a loan for consumption (*mutuum*) *there is no just* cause for profit by reason of the contract itself, the present canon states implicitly that in modern times there is always present in such a loan some just reason for demanding the legal rate of interest and explicitly allows an even greater

63 Canon 1541,§§2-3.

64 Canon 1543.

rate of interest provided there be just and proportionate reasons for demanding it. The canon, however, studiously avoids determining what these just reasons are, leaving that to the Catholic moralists and economists to determine.[65]

ARTICLE 2. NEVADA LAW ON ADMINISTRATION

Administration of church property in Nevada will be determined in part by the act under which a particular Church or religious society has incorporated in the state. The rights and duties of trustees and administrators are outlined in these incorporating acts; further rights and duties, not in conflict with the laws of Nevada, may be contained in the articles of incorporation. In the administration of trusts, testamentary or nontestamentary, the powers and obligations of the trustee may be explicitly named in the instrument creating the trust. Such a trustee is also governed by the laws of Nevada covering such trusts. Further, the whole matter of sale, exchange, mortgaging, leasing, loans, etc. will be conducted under the Nevada statutes governing these various contracts. These civil laws on contracts have canonical force for Church administrators, as well as civil force, by reason of the canonization of the civil law on contracts in canon 1529.[66] Nevada law on these contracts is far too extensive to be included in this work. However, some comment is in order on the general powers and obligations of administrators of church property, liability of religious corporations, tax exemptions granted to church property and zoning laws.

Section I. Powers and Obligations of Administrators

In the corporation sole act, Nevada law has conveyed the widest possible freedom to churches in Nevada in the administration of their property. Churches so incorporated may, without the order of any court, buy, sell, lease, and mortgage their property. The statute states that they may deal in real and personal property in the same manner that a natural person may.[67] Accordingly, the Roman Catholic Bishop of Reno, as a corporation sole, is granted full administrative power over all the property which belongs to the corporation. His duties and rights in the administration of the property of the diocese of Reno are the same as those of a natural person. In other

[65] p. 845.
[66] Cf. *supra*, p. 118.
[67] NRS. 84.050; Cf. *supra*, pp. 43, 99.

words, Bishop Dwyer of Reno today has the same rights and duties in regard to the property of the Church in Nevada as he has towards his own private property. Of course, he will always maintain full administrative power over his privately owned property, but he will continue to exercise his full administrative power over the church property only so long as he continues to be the corporation sole. His successor as the Roman Catholic Bishop of Reno will succeed to the full administrative power over the church property, whereas he can dispose of his privately owned property by last will and testament, as he sees fit.

The Nevada statute grants the bishop, as the corporation sole, the power to grant, sell, convey, rent, or otherwise dispose of the property of the Church. He is given the right to borrow money and to give promissory notes or some other written obligation therefore, and to secure payment thereof by mortgage or other lien upon real or personal property. He can receive bequests and devises for his own use as the corporation sole, and also upon trusts, in the same way that natural persons may. He can appoint attorneys in fact. He can contract and be contracted with, sue and be sued, plead and be pleaded against in all court of justice. He can have and use a common seal by which all deeds and acts are authenticated.[68] In executing deeds and other instruments in writing, the Nevada statute requires the bishop to execute them in the name of the corporation and to sign them as the representative of the corporation. They must be sealed with the seal of the corporation. An impression of this seal must be filed in the office of the secretary of state.[69]

Thus the bishop's administrative powers are as wide as those of any natural person. He has freedom to care for the goods of the Church according to the rules of canon law. The state does not interfere in or curtail his rights of administration in its corportion sole laws. However, by this type of incorporation all the property of the diocese is lumped together. Thus, the debts incurred by one parish or institution are legally the debts of the corporation sole. Accordingly, the property of one parish can be taken from it in order to pay the debts of another parish. Canon law envisions each parish as a separate entity in holding and administering church property. The state recognizes only the corporation sole, and sees each parish only as a part of that corporation. There is no distinction made bet-

[68] NRS. 84.050.
[69] NRS. 84.060.

ween the property of one parish and that of another. One parish is liable for any act of any other parish in the diocese. This view of church property is not only uncanonical, but could work an unfair burden on the members of one parish by forcing them to use their funds to meet the obligations of some other parish in the diocese, which may be hundreds of miles away. To help another parish out of charity is a praiseworthy act, but to make the property of one parish equally the property of another as far as legal obligations are concerned is an unfair burden. This imposes the added duty on bishops to watch most carefully that the rights of one parish are not thus imposed upon by the obligations of another.

Churches which are incorporated under the 1867 act, which provides for the incorporation or religious, charitable, literary, scientific, and other associations, do not have such full administrative powers as are granted by the corporation sole act. The trustees or directors of these corporations may take into their possession and custody all the temporalities of the corporation. They may sue and be sued. They may receive and hold all the debts, demands, rights and privileges, and also all churches, burying places, halls, schoolhouses, hospitals and other buildings, as well as all estates and appurtenances belonging to the association or society. They have the power to lease and improve these properties. They may also erect all houses and buildings which are needed to carry out the objects of the society or association. The statute further gives them the general right to perform all duties which are imposed upon them by the regulations, rules or discipline of the organization.

However, the trustees or directors of these corporations must obtain the approval of the district court for the sale of any real estate belonging to the association or society. The court shall also direct the application of the moneys arising from such sale to such uses as the corporation or association, with the court's approval, shall deem to be for the best interests of the corporation or association. A court order is also needed by the trustees or directors in order to mortgage, hypothecate, or give a deed of trust upon any of the real estate of the society. Thus the administration of the trustees or directors of churches which are incorporated under this act is limited by the statute. This act also contains a mortmain law, limiting the amount of property which churches incorporated under it can hold.[70]

[70] NRS. 86.120-86.130, and 86.160. Cf. *supra,* pp. 107-109 for details on the Mortmain statute.

In conveying or encumbering lands, tenements and hereditaments of the association, the trustees or directors are empowered by the statute to do so either in their own names or in the corporate name of the association. The law requires the trustees to make an annual report to the society or association concerning all the real and personal property held in trust by them, and concerning the general condition of the corporation. A copy of this report must be filed in the office of the county clerk where the original certificate of incorporation is filed. It is to be accompanied by an affidavit attesting its truth and the fact that the corporation has not been engaged, directly or indirectly, in any business other than that described in the original certificate on file.[71]

Section II. Liability

The question of the tort liability of religious and charitable societies has proved to be a particularly difficult one in Anglo-American jurisprudence. The courts of the various states have differed widely in their interpretations on the matter, some holding churches liable for the torts of their servants and agents and others exempting churches from all tort liability. Indeed, courts within the same state have reversed themselves in that matter.

In general, it may be said that formerly the majority of decisions exempted churches from the torts of their agents and servants. However, the trend today is decidedly in the opposite direction.

This general shift in the attitude of civil law towards the tort liability of churches is evidenced in Nevada law. As recently as 1955, in the case of Springer vs. Federated Church of Reno,[72] the Nevada supreme court held that, although the member of the church was delivering a card file regarding church membership when she fell while descending the church steps, she was a beneficiary of the church, and as such could not recover damages from the church in a personal injury action based on negligence. The court in this case followed the old beneficiary theory limiting tort liability of charitable organizations, adhering to the rule under the doctrine of *stare decisis*.

However, the Nevada legislature in 1957, perhaps acting because of this decision, wrote a new liability law into the Nevada

[71] NRS. 86.140, 86.170.

[72] Springer vs. Federated Church of Reno, 71 Nev. 177, 253 Pac. 2d. 1071

statutes. This new statute holds that no nonprofit corporation, association, or organization shall be immune from liability for the injury or damage caused any person, firm, or corporation as a result of the negligent or wrongful act of such nonprofit corporation, association, or act of its agents, employees, or servants acting within the scope of their agency or employment.[73] This law leaves no doubt about the tort liability of churches. Under its provision all churches, even unincorporated ones, will be liable for the torts of its agents, employees, or servants, when they are acting within the scope of their agency or employment. This puts churches on the same basis as all other organizations in the matter of tort liability, and marks a decided change of attitude towards churches in the matter.

One explanation for this changing attitude toward the tort liability of churches is the following:

> The rule of exemption from liability arose when charitable organizations, having their origin in donations of benevolent persons or in grants from the state, were supported by a few individuals and their resources were limited. It was, therefore, in the best interests of the public that such institutions were nurtured. Today charity is dispensed by large well-endowed corporations, whose modern multiplication has apparently reduced this danger and rendered more equitable the payment of compensation to those so injured. Thus the demands of the public welfare, for protection from liabilities for wrongs committed in their conduct, have become less imperative as compared with the needs of the injured individual. Their economic aspects are nonprofit rather than charitable.[74]

Another consideration, not mentioned by Larber but indicated in his remarks, is the fact that religious and charitable organizations are heavily insured today. The question of insurance has definitely had an effect on the increased amounts allowed for damages by the courts in recent times. The fact of insurance has removed the need of immunity by religious and charitable corporations and groups from tort liability and may be considered a major factor in the new trend of the legislatures and courts in this matter.

(1955).

[73] NRS. 41.480.

[74] Larber, "Liability of Hospitals for the Negligence of Their Employees," *St. John's Law Review*, XV (1941), 276-277.

A recent decision by a New York Court of Appeals demonstrates the forcefulness of the new thinking on this question, when it declares:

> Hospitals should, in short, shoulder the responsibilities borne by everyone else. There is no reason to continue their exemption from the universal rule of *respondeat superior.* The test should be for these institutions, whether charitable or profit-making, as it is for every other employer, was the person who committed the negligent injury-producing act one of its employees and, if he was, was he acting within the scope of his employment.
>
> The rule of non-liability is out of tune with the life about us, at variance with modern-day needs and concepts of justice and fair dealing. It should be discarded.[75]

Here the court did not consider whether the act of the employee was administrative or medical in order to determine whether immunity should be allowed, but rather, acting on the principle that immunity should not be allowed in either case, considered only whether the act was one of an employee acting within the scope of employment.

While decisions are still being handed down, granting immunity to religious and charitable organizations, notably in Texas, the general trend all across the country is to refuse this immunity today. The explicitness of the 1957 statute in Nevada law leaves no doubt about the question for churches and all other nonprofit organizations in that state.

Section III. Taxation

The exemption of religious and charitable organizations from taxation is a universal practice in the United States, although the extent of the exemptions differs among the various states. The constitutions of the various states may be divided into three classes with regard to the tax exemption granted to churches. Some state constitutions are silent on the matter; a second group of state constitutions contain self-executing provisions; a third group grant their legislatures express powers to pass exemption statutes. This third group may be further divided into those constitutions which leave the matter of exemption entirely to the discretion of the legislature and those which say that the legislature *shall* pass such exemptions

[75] Bing vs. Thunig, 2 N.Y. 2d. 656, 143 N.E. 2d. (1957).

but leave it to their discretion to determine the extent of the exemptions.[76]

In states where the constitution is silent on the matter the legislatures have passed statutes granting such exemptions, acting on the basis that they have received the power to so exempt from immemorial usage.[77] Self-executing constitutional provisions are beyond the powers of the legislatures to change, unless the provision gives the legislature the power to supersede it. They can be changed only by a change in the constitution itself and thus have the support and steadfastness of the highest law-making power known to our system of government. The constitutional provisions which grant the legislature the power to pass these tax exemptions are powers of attorney rather than laws themselves; they authorize the legislatures to act but do not grant the exemption constitutionally. However, some of these constitutional provisions command that some exemption must be passed by the legislature; others merely state that the legislature *may* so act.

The state of Nevada ranks among these last named states. The Nevada constitution provides:

> All real property, and possessory rights to the same, as well as personal property in this State, belonging to corporations now existing or hereafter created shall be subject to taxation, the same as property of individuals; *Provided, that the property of corporations formed for Municipal, Charitable, Religious, or Educational purposes may be exempted by law* (italics mine).[78]

Another constitutional provision, which instructs the legislature to provide by law for a uniform and equal rate of assessment and taxation, adds that "there shall also be excepted such property as *may* be exempted by law for municipal, educational, literary, scientific or other charitable purposes."[79]

Thus the Nevada constitution, by the use of the word *may* has given the legislature the power to exempt these various groups from taxation at its own discretion. Churches in Nevada, then, are not guaranteed tax exemption by the constitution, but are dependent upon

[76] Zollman, p. 330-332.
[77] *Ibid.*, p. 332.
[78] Art. VIII, Sec. 2.
[79] Art. X, Sec. I.

laws which may or may not be passed by the legislature to gain such exemptions.

Nevada legislatures have been constant and broad in granting such tax exemptions. They have passed laws exempting from taxation: churches, chapels, buildings used for religious worship, their furniture, equipment, and the lots of ground on which they stand and their parsonages; cemeteries; the funds, furniture, and regalia of lodges and other charitable organizations; the buildings and lands of charitable corporations; nonprofit, private schools with their furniture, equipment, and lots appurtenant thereto.[80]

Provisions granting tax exemptions to churches, both those granted by constitutions and those granted by statutes, fall into two classes. Some states exempt the property of churches from taxation regardless of the use to which that property is put. Other states determine the exemption by the purpose for which the property is used.[81] Nevada falls into the second class. In granting tax exemptions to churches and chapels the law provides that "when any such property is used exclusively or in part for any other than church purposes, and a rent or other valuable consideration is received for its use, the same shall be taxed."[82]

It should be noted that the Nevada law expressly exempts the houses of priests and ministers from taxation. The statute exempting nonprofit private schools mentions the lots appurtenant thereto, thus exempting school playgrounds. However, the law is not explicit in the matter of lots which may be bought by a church and not used, such as property bought for the purpose of building at some future date, when the funds for such construction become available. Some states expressly exempt such vacant, unused lots; however, most states hold that vacant land held by the Church as an investment is not in use for any religious purpose and therefore not tax exempt.[83] Nevada law fails to mention such property expressly, and since ex-

[80] NRS. 361.105 and 361.125-361.140.

[81] Cooley, *The Law of Taxation* (4 vols., Vol. II, 4ed., Chicago, 1924), II, 1553-1554.

[82] NRS. 361.125. This statute also excepts marriage chapels from the exemption, apparently inasmuch as marriage is looked upon more as a business in Nevada than a part of religion and in fact marriage chapels are built and operated in Nevada, notably in Reno and Las Vegas, primarily as business enterprises.

[83] "Exemption of Property Owned by Religious Organizations," *Minnesota Law Review*, XI (1927), 548.

emption statutes generally receive a strict construction,[84] it seems that such land could be taxed in that state. On the other hand since the law expressly states that church property is to be taxed when used for other than church purposes, it could be argued that its temporary lack of any use was never intended by the Nevada lawmakers as an excuse to tax it. However, the question must remain in doubt, since it has not yet been proposed to the Nevada courts. They might follow a New York precedent in taking the view that the importance to the public of religious, charitable, and educational activities warrants a relaxation of the ordinary rule that exemption provisions be strictly construed.[85] The State of New York has an express statute on this matter, in which it rules that vacant lots are not to be taxed if construction of buildings or improvements are in progress or are in good faith contemplated.[86] The addition of such a clause to the Nevada statute would clarify this problem, and in these times, when the high cost of construction often delays or postpones its execution, is highly recommended.

Nevada law also exempts from the state sales tax "any organization created for religious, charitable or eleemosynary purposes, provided that no part of the net earnings of any such organization inures to the benefit of any private shareholders or individual."[87]

Section IV. Zoning Laws

Municipal zoning laws apply to religious and charitable corporations as well as to individuals. Thus, in erecting church property these particular laws of municipalities must be observed by church administrators and trustees. However, such laws cannot in their building limitations disregard the basic rights to freedom guaranteed by the federal and state constitutions. Zoning laws are passed as a part of the police power of the state and as such must bear "some substantial relationship to the public health, safety, morals, or general welfare," and must cease "when they encroach on the protection accorded the citizen by the Federal Constitution."[88]

Thus in Roman Catholic Bishop of Reno vs. Hill[89] the supreme court declared invalid those sections of the Reno zoning ordinance

84 Zollman, p. 333.

85 St. Barbara's Roman Catholic Church vs. New York, 243 App. Div. 371, 373, 277 N.Y.S. 538, 541 (2d Dept., (1935); Cf. Murphy, p. 94.

86 Murphy, p. 93.

87 NRS. 372.325.

88 Women's Kansas City St. Andrew Soc. vs. Kansas City, Mo., 8 Civ., 58 F. 2d.

which require the written permission of 75 per cent of the owners of property within a certain distance for the construction of a building in a residential district for nonresidential purposes, when they were applied to the building of Our Lady of Snows Church. The court said these sections, so applied, were invalid as violations of the due process clause of State and Federal Constitutions. The court stated in this case:

> The validity of Sections 7 and 8 of the Zoning Ordinance has been challenged on several grounds, but we have found it necessary to consider but one. The great weight of authority convinces us that these sections, as applied to the property involved in this case, bear no substantial relationship to the promotion of the health, safety, morals, convenience, property or general welfare of the City of Reno, or of its Residential District, and that they constitute an invasion of the property rights of petitioner corporation.

Of historical interest are the remarks of the court concerning the conduct of funerals:

> Respondent urges that funerals at the proposed new church would have a depressing effect on near-by residents; but it is a matter of common knowledge that funeral services are frequently conducted in the finest as well as the less pretentious private homes in the residential district of the city . . . Death is a part of our existence and is as natural as life. We are unable to perceive why a church funeral service, reverently conducted as such services uniformly are, should have a more depressing effect on normal persons than one held at a private residence.

593 (1932).

[89] Roman Catholic Bishop of Reno vs. Hill, 59 Nev. 231, 90 Pac. 2d 217 (1939).

CONCLUSIONS

The Catholic Church and all other religious societies have been afforded ample freedom and protection in the State of Nevada, so that they have been able to grow and flourish in this state unencumbered by civil restrictions or opposition. The Church in Nevada is developing stride for stride with the State itself. (pp. 1-23)

The Catholic Church and the Apostolic See enjoy moral personality by divine institution. Other moral persons in the Church receive their personality from ecclesiastical authority either by a provision of law or by a formal decree. In the United States, Nevada included, the legal personality of the Church as such is not admitted. However, for purposes of acquiring, holding, and administering property, religious, charitable, and educational corporations may be created through application of corporation statutes enacted for those purposes. (pp. 24-47)

Among the various corporation laws in Nevada two have special reference for the purposes of churches. These are the act of 1867 which provides for the incorporation of religious, charitable, literary, scientific, and other associations, and the corporation sole act of 1915. (pp. 96-97)

The 1867 act bears certain similarities to the parish corporation act, recommended by the Sacred Congregation of the Council. However, it contains a limitation as to sales and mortgages, an unjust mortmain law, and accounting requirements, which make it an undersirable law for the incorporation of Roman Catholic Churches. (pp. 103-109)

The Diocese of Reno is incorporated in Nevada under the corporation sole act of 1915. The Roman Catholic Bishop of Reno and His Successors, A Corporation Sole is the name under which the diocese is incorporated and through which all church property under diocesan control is held and administered. This form of incorporation, while receiving only secondary approval by the Sacred Congregation of the Council, in practice affords the Bishop of Reno freedom to apply the rules of canon law concerning church property. (pp. 85-92, 97-103)

If a change in the method of tenure of its property by the Catholic Church in Nevada were desired, there is ample precedent in Nevada legislation of specific corporation laws providing for the incorporation of particular groups, for the Church to seek and expect passage of an act providing for the incorporation of Roman Catholic Dioceses, Churches, and Institutions. (pp. 109-110)

The Catholic Church in Nevada can acquire property by donations *inter vivos,* bequests and devises in last wills and testaments, and adverse possession of sacred things and other church property, both as regards their prescriptibility and the time required for their prescription, are not protected by the civil law of Nevada. (pp. 72-82)

The Code of Canon Law names the Roman Pontiff the supreme legislator and dispenser of all ecclesiastical goods. Bishops are given the duty of diligently supervising the administration of the esslesiastical goods in their respective territories.

According to the norms of canon law, they are the immediate administrators of that church property which constitutes the episcopal benefice, funds held in common for the benefit of the diocese, the diocesan seminary, and the property of the cathedral church. However, Nevada law through its corporation sole law makes the bishop the administrator of all the property of the corporation. The civil law does not prevent the bishop from allowing pastors and rectors of churches freedom to carry on the ordinary administration intended by the norms of the Code. Administrative powers granted in the corporation sole act are broader than those given in the act of 1867. Nevada law holds churches liable for the torts of their agents, servants and employees when acting within the scope of their agency or employment. Nevada's tax exemption laws are statutory in nature and grant broad exemptions to churches. Zoning laws of municipalities are upheld in Nevada, unless they violate the constitutional rights of the Church. (pp. 111-134)

BIBLIOGRAPHY

Sources

Acta Apostolicae Sedis, Commentarium Officiale, Romae, 1909-1929 Civitate Vaticana, 1929-

Acta et Decreta Concelii Plenarii Baltimorensis Tertii, A. D. MDCCCLXXXIV. Baltimorae: Typis Joannis Murphy et Sociorum, 1886.

Articles of Incorporation of the Roman Catholic Bishop of Reno, And His Successors, A Corporation Sole, a certified copy dated at Reno, February 20, 1959.

Canon Law Digest, The, 4 vols., Milwaukee: Bruce Publishing Co., Vol. I, 1934, Vol. II, 1943, Vol. III, 1954, edited by T. Lincoln Bouscaren; Vol. IV, 1958, edited by T. Lincoln Bouscaren and James I. O'Connor.

Codex Iuris Canonici, Pii X Pontificis Maximi iussu digestus, Benedicti Papae XV auctoritate promulgatus, Romae: Typis Polyglottis Vaticanis, 1917.

Compiled Laws of Nevada, The, In Force from 1861 to 1900 (Inclusive), Carson City: Andrew Maute, Superintendent of State Printing, 1900, compiled by Henry C. Cutting.

Compiled Laws, The, State of Nevada, embracing Statutes of 1861 to 1873, Inclusive, 2 vols., Carson City: Charles A. V. Putnam, State Printer 1873, compiled by M. S. Bonnifield and T. W. Healy.

Concilii Plenarii Baltimorensis II in Ecclesia Metropolitana Baltimorensis a die VII ad diem XXI Octobris A.D. MDCCLXVI habiti et a Sede Apostolica Recogniti Acta et Decreta, 2 ed., Baltimore: John Murphy, 1880.

Corpus Iuris Canonici, edition Lipsiensis secunda, post Aemilii Richteri curas . . . instruxit Aemilius Friedberg, 2 vols., Lipsiae, 1879-1881.

Corpus Iuris Secundum, 95 Vols. and Indices, Brooklyn, N.Y.: The American Law Book Co., 1936-1951.

Diocese of Reno, First Synod, Reno, Nevada: 1958.

General Statutes of the State of Nevada, The, in force from 1861-1885 Inclusive, Carson City: Josiah C. Harlow, Superintendent of State Printing, 1885, compiled by David E. Baily and John D. Hammond.

Hardouin, Joannes, *Acta Conciliorum et Epistolae Decretales,* 12 vols., Parisilis, 1715.

Mansi, Joannes, *Sacrorum Conciliorum Nova et Amplissima Collectio,* 53 vols. in 60, Parisilis, 1901-1927.

Nevada Compiled Laws 1929, 6 vols., San Francisco: Bender-Moss Company 1930, compiled by Curtis Hillyer.

Nevada Revised Statutes, 6 vols., Carson City: 1957, Russell W. McDonald, Director, Statute Revision Commission.

Revised Laws of Nevada, containing State Statutes of a General Nature from 1861 Revised to 1912, 2 vols., Carson City: Joe Farnsworth, Superintendent of State Printing, 1912, revised by James G. Sweeney, G. F. Talbot, F. H. Norcross.

State of Nevada, Report and Official Opinions of the Attorney General, for the Period, July 1, 1948, to June 30, 1950, Inclusive, Carson City: State Printing Office, Jack McCarthy, Superintendent, 1950.

Reference Works

Abbo, J. - Hannan, J., *The Sacred Canons: A Concise Presentation of the Current Disciplinary Norms of the Church,* 2 vols., St. Louis: B. Herder Book Company, 1952.

Augustine, Charles, *A Commentary on the New Code of Canon Law,* 8 vols., Vol. VI, 3.ed., St. Louis: B. Herder Book Co., 1923.

Ayrinhac, H. A., *Administrative Legislation in the New Code of Canon Law,* London, New York, Toronto: Longmans, Green & Co., 1928.

Bancroft, Hubert H., *The Works of Hubert Bancroft,* 39 vols., San Francisco, Vol. XXV, The History Company, 1890. *History of Nevada, Colorado, and Wyoming.*

Bartlett, Chester, J. *The Tenure of Parochial Property in the United States of America,* The Catholic University of America Canon Law Studies, n. 31. Washington, D.C.: The Catholic University of America Press, 1926.

Black, Henry Campbell, *Black's Law Dictionary,* 3.ed., St. Paul: West Publishing Co., 1933.

Blackstone, William, *Commentaries on the Laws of England,* annotated by George Sharswood, 4 vols. in 2, Philadelphia: J. B. Lippincott Co., 1898.

Bouscaren, T. Lincoln - Ellis, Adam C., *Canon Law: A Text and Commentary,* 2. revised ed., Milwaukee: Bruce Publishing Co., 1951.

Brown, Brendan, *The Canonical Juristic Personality with Special Reference to its Status in the United States of America,* The Catholic University of America Canon and Civil Law Studies, n. 39, Washington, D.C.; The Catholic University of America Press, 1927.

Byrne, Harry, J., *Investment of Church Funds: A Study in Administrative Law,* The Catholic University of America Canon Law Studies, n. 309, Washington, D.C.: The Catholic University of America Press, 1951.

Cappelo, Felix, *Summa Iuris Canonici,* 3 vols., Vol. II, 4.ed., Romae: Apud Aedes Universitatis Gregorianae, 1945.

Cavagnis, Felix, *Institutiones Iuris Publicis Ecclesiastici,* 3 vols., Romae: 1906.

Cleary, Joseph F., *Canonical Limitations on the Alienation of Church Property,* The Catholic University of America Canon Law Studies, n. 100, Washington, D.C.: The Catholic University of America Press, 1936.

Cooley, Thomas, *The Law of Taxation,* 4 vols., Vol. II, 4.ed., Chicago, 1924.

Coronata, M. Conte, *Institutiones Iuris Canonici,* 5 vols., Vol. I, 4.ed., 1950: 4.ed., 1950; Vol. II, 4.ed., 1951, Taurini-Romae: Marietti.

DeMeester, Alphonsus, *Iuris Canonici et Iuris Canonico-Civilis Compendium,* nova ed., 3 vols. in 4, Brugis: Descles, 1921-1928.

Dignan, Patrick J., *A History of the Legal Incorporation of Catholic Church Property in the United States,* New York: Kennedy & Sons, 1935.

Doheny, William J., Church Property: *Modes of Acquisition,* The Catholic University of America Canon and Roman Law Studies, n. 41, Washington, D.C.: The Catholic University of America Press, 1927.

Goodwine, John A., *The Right of the Church to Acquire Temporal Goods,* The Catholic University of America Canon Law Studies, n. 131, Washington, D.C.: The Catholic University of America Press, 1941.

Gorman, Thomas K., *Seventy-Five Years of Catholic Life in Nevada,* Reno: The Journal Press, 1935.

Haddan, A. W.-Stubbs, W., *Councils and Ecclesiastical Documents Relating to Great Britain and Ireland,* 3 vols., Vol. III, Oxford, 1869-1873.

Kremer, Michael, *Church Support in the United States,* The Catholic University of America Canon Law Studies, n. 61, Washington, D.C.: The Catholic University of America Press, 1930.

Mack, Effie Mona, *Nevada,* Glendale, California: The Arthur H. Clark Co., 1936.

Martin, Thomas O., *Adverse Possession, Prescription and Limitation of Actions. The Canonical "Praescriptio,"* The Catholic University of America Canon Law Studies, n. 202, Washington, D.C.: The Catholic University of America Press, 1944.

Michiels, Gommarus, *Principia Generalia de Personis in Ecclesia,* 2.ed., Parisilis-Tornaic-Romae: Desclee, 1955.

Morgan, Dale L.,*The Humboldt: Highroad of the West,* New York: Farrar-Rinehart, 1934.

Murphy, Joseph P., *The Laws of the State of New York Affecting Church Property,* The Catholic University of America Canon Law Studies, n. 388, Washington, D.C.: The Catholic University of America Press, 1957.

Ottaviani, A., *Institutiones Juris Publici Ecclesiastici,* 2 vols., 3.ed., Romae: Typis Polyglottis Vaticanis, 1947-1948.

Scheys, Carolus, *De Iure Ecclesiae Acquirendi et Possidendi Bona Temporalia,* Louvain: 1892.

Tarquini, Camillus, *Iuris Ecclesiastici Publici Institutiones,* 4.ed., Romae: 1875.

Thompson, Thomas H. West, Albert A., *History of Nevada,* Berkeley: Howell-North, 1881, a Reproduction with Illustration and Biographical sketches of its Prominent men and Pioneers, Berkeley: Howell and North, 1958.

Vermeersch, A. - Creusen, J., *Epitome Iuris Canonici,* 3 vols., Vol. II, 7.ed., Mechliniae-Romae: H. Dessain, 1949.

Vromant, G., *De Bonis Ecclesiae Temporalibus,* 3.ed., Burges-Paris: Desclee de Brouwer, 1953.

Wernz, Franciscus X., *Ius Decretalium,* 6 vols., Romae: 1898-1914.

Wiggins, Urban C., *Property Laws of the State of Ohio Affecting Church Property,* The Catholic University of America Canon Law Studies, n. 367, Washington, D.C.: The Catholic University of America Press, 1956.

Woywod, S. - Smith, C., *A Practical Commentary on the Code of Canon Law,* 2 vols., revised by Callistus Smith, revised and enlarged edition, New York: Joseph F. Wagner, Inc., 1948.

Zollman, Carl, *American Civil Church Law,* Columbia University Studies in History, Economics, and Public Law, Vol. 77, New York: Columbia University and Longmans, Green & Co., 1917.

———, "Exemption of Property Owned or Used by Religious Organizations." *Minnesota Law Review,* XI (1927), 541-551.

Larber, Harry, "Liability of Hospitals for the Negligence of Their Employers," *St. John's Law Review,* XV (1941), 275-283.

McGrath, John J., " Canon Law and American Church Law: A Comparative Study," *The Jurist,* XVIII (1958), 260-278.

Zollman, Carl, "Powers of American Religious Corporations," *Michigan Law Review,* XIII (1915), 646-666.

Periodicals

Jurist, The, Washington, D.C. 1941—

Michigan Law Review, Ann Arbor, 1902—

Minnesota Law Review, Minneapolis, 1916—

Nevada Register, The, Reno, 1935—

St. John's Law Review, Brooklyn, 1926—

ABBREVIATIONS

B—Bonnifield and Healy, *The Compiled Laws of the State of Nevada* (*1873*).

BH—Baily and Hammond, *The General Statutes of the State of Nevada* (*1885*).

C—Cutting, *Compiled Laws of Nevada* (*1900*).

NCL—*Nevada Compiled Laws* (*1929*).

NRS—*Nevada Revised Statutes.*

RL—*Revised Laws of Nevada* (*1912*).

INDEX OF AMERICAN CASES CITED

(Numbers refer to page numbers herein)

ALPHABETICAL INDEX

BIOGRAPHICAL NOTE

Maurice Laurence Welsh was born October 12, 1922, in Yerington, Nevada. After graduating from St. Thomas Aquinas Parochial school in Reno, Nevada, he entered the preparatory seminary, St. Joseph's College, Mountain View, California, in 1936. He entered St. Patrick's Seminary, Menlo Park, California in 1942, receiving a Bachelor of Arts degree in 1944. He was ordained a priest for the Diocese of Reno on April 5, 1947. After serving as an assistant pastor at St. Thomas Aquinas Cathedral, he entered the University of Nevada and in June, 1949, received the Bachelor of Arts in Journalism degree. After attending summer school at Fordham University, New York, he worked at the News Service of the National Catholic Welfare Conference, Washington, D.C., while taking editorial background courses at the Catholic University of America. He became editor of the *Nevada Register* in 1950. The Denver School of Journalism granted him a Master of Arts degree in 1956, and in Sepember of the same year he was admitted to the School of Canon Law of the Catholic University of America. He received the Baccalaureate Degree in Canon Law in June, 1957, and the Licentiate Degree in Canon Law in June, 1958.

CANON LAW STUDIES *

402. Chyang, Rev. Peter B., M.A., J.C.L., Decennial faculties for ordinaries in quasi-dioceses.

403. Gossman, Rev. Francis J., A.B., S.T.L., J.C.L., Pope Urban II and canon law.

404. Love, Rev. Paul L., A.B., J.C.L., The penal remedies of the Code.

405. McLeaish, Rev. Donald C., A.B., S.T.L., J.C.L., The laws of the State of Texas affecting church property.

406. Rodriquez, Rev. Manuel J., Ph.B., S.T.L., J.C.L., The laws of the State of New Mexico affecting church property.

407. Sampon, Rev. Robert G., Ph.B., S.T.L., J.C.L., A comparative study of the First Provincial Council of Milwaukee and the Code of Canon Law.

408. Schreiber, Rev. Paul F., A.B., J.C.L., Canonical precedence.

409. Welsh, Rev. Maurice L., A.B., M.A., J.C.L., The laws of the State of Nevada affecting church property.

* For a complete list of the available members of this series apply to the Catholic University of America Press, 620 Michigan Ave., N.E., Washington (17), D.C., for a general catalogue.

www.ingramcontent.com/pod-product-compliance
Lightning Source LLC
LaVergne TN
LVHW050223080826
844660LV00012B/458

* 9 7 8 0 8 1 3 2 2 5 6 8 5 *